Reversible Skirt

Reversible Skirt

A Memoir

Laura McHale Holland

Wordforest
Rohnert Park, California

Reversible Skirt
© 2011 by Laura McHale Holland

ISBN: 978-0-9829365-0-4

Library of Congress Control Number: 2010941423

First printing: March 2011
10 9 8 7 6 5 4 3 2 1

This book is distributed by Ingram Book Group and Baker & Taylor.

Cover design by Kathy McHale at McHale Creative
www.mchalecreative.com.

Author photo by Jason Figueroa
www.photography-by-jason.com.

Note: To respect privacy, the names and, in some cases, identifying
characteristics of many people mentioned in this book have been
changed, author's family excepted.

For my parents, Hank and Mary Agnes,
whose high hopes brought me into this world.

It was an accident. Not the suicide. I planned that, although there are some things I would change if I were to do it over now. But the mess after the suicide, that was the accident. Amoebic anxiety dividing and rising like yeast in my husband's lower intestine, grief unattended pouring wet cement into the pauses of my children's games, the replacement wife/mother hiding every picture of me in paper bags taped shut and marked, "Do not touch. Alligators inside." I never intended all of that. I thought things would be more bearable if my family were spared my madness. And I thought I would return in penance to our Holy Father.

I was wrong.

Mary Agnes

Gramma

Gramma loves me. I know this by the way she says my name, Laura. She lilts it, tickles the air with it, like I'm a ruby she's just spied glittering in one of the sidewalk cracks in front of her great big red brick apartment building. It's on Birchwood Avenue. And that's where I am right now. Looking out the parlor window. Waiting. It's like I'm standing on a mountain of cream puffs all mine alone because any minute Gramma will call my name and tell me it's time for our special ride. Nobody else says my name the way Gramma does. Not Daddy, not Kathy and Mary Ruth, not Uncle John, and not Mommy, who loves church so much I think maybe she up and moved into one a while back.

Daddy has two ways of saying my name. The first is like it's the punch line to a joke that only he understands, a joke that jiggles him up tall almost all the way out of his shiny black shoes. He looks at me with his gray eyes sparkling like a silver spoon with all the tarnish wiped off. When he's happy like that, he calls me "Shimp," which he says is shrimp and imp put together, or he says "Laura Fadora Fadoo." He stretches that doo out real long like the last note of a song,

1

and then Kathy and Mary Ruth turn it into "Laura Kapora Kapoo." They stretch the poo out just as long, and just like that, all the fun of having him say my name is gone.

The second way Daddy says my name is like a ball he's thrown really hard to get my attention because he wants me to stop doing whatever it is I'm doing. When he says my name this way his face looks harder than the sides of Gramma's building, and the last thing I want is to scrape up against him. The second is the way he says my name most often. And that makes me mad, but I'm not supposed to ever get mad at Daddy.

Now when Daddy's around, which isn't all that often, and when he's not stretched out asleep with his dark hair mixing in with the tatters of Gramma's soft green couch, he's making a commotion. He's like pots and pans falling from Gramma's kitchen cupboards, knocking against the stove and table and chairs and banging hard on the wooden patches in the floor where the old linoleum is worn clear off. He echoes all through the building like thunder. But Daddy all the time tells me, "Laura, be quiet! Laura, settle down! Be a good girl now, Laura!" He has to throw my name around a lot to hammer this idea home; it's about as hard to be quiet as it is to keep my Cracker Jacks from falling out of the box when I open it and turn it upside down looking for the charm hidden inside.

My sisters, Kathy and Mary Ruth, have their blond heads glued together most of the time whispering. And sometimes they set their deep blue eyes on me and say my name either right at the same time or one after the other like echoes in a tunnel. Their lips are moving, but my name seems to come out of their noses like when you snort your milk instead of swallowing it, and it burns going through your nostrils until you spurt it out, finally, and you're not at all pleased. That's Kathy and Mary Ruth, not at all pleased when they say, "Laura peed in her pants, Gramma," or "Laura's eating bouillon cubes again, Gramma," or "Laura can't sing the ABC song yet, Gramma."

But they always include me in games, morning to night, like me or not. They never tell me I can't play. The first thing we usually do is ride trikes. We have two red ones, all dented and scratched up, and one green one a little bigger and newer, but still pretty banged up too. The green one is mine. I got it for my second birthday, which was way long ago because Gramma says now I'm going on three years old. It was a thrill when Daddy set it down on the sidewalk for the first time and lifted me onto the marshmallow white seat. Oh, what a beauty! The handlebars and body of the trike were deep green; the grips were green and white striped and there were green and white streamers coming out of a little hole in the end of each grip. The tires were all firm and darkest black, and the spokes of the wheels were gleaming in the sunshine. My trike, my very own trike. I couldn't wait to ride it. Until this moment I could only ride one of the red trikes if Kathy and Mary Ruth didn't want it first because they were their trikes, not mine. They had first dibs.

So there I was on my ride. My pride fanned out around me like a great big peacock tail. I gripped the handlebars and stretched my legs. I could reach the top pedal, but the lower one was way beyond reach.

"Look, Daddy, she can't ride it," said Kathy.

"Yeah, it's too big for her," Mary Ruth added.

"Looks like you're right, girls. Maybe one of you should give it a try," Daddy said, lifting me off the trike.

"No! No! No!" I shrieked. "My trike. My trike."

"Oh, settle down, Laura" Daddy said, "What good will it do just sitting on the sidewalk?"

Daddy put me down and turned around, taking a few steps toward Gramma's front door. Kathy and Mary Ruth raced to the new trike, shoving each other and screaming.

"Lemme," cried Mary Ruth.

"No. Lemme," cried Kathy.

I ran to the trike and held on hard to one of the handlebars.

"Mine, mine!" I yelled.

Kathy was holding the other handlebar, and Mary Ruth had hold of the seat. We were kicking and spitting up a storm. Each of us had one hand on the trike and with the free hand was trying to pry the other two off. But each of us was holding her ground.

Daddy spun around, "Stop it, you three. Stop fighting right now," he commanded.

We were so worked up. We heard him, but kept right on batting and clawing. I had just gotten my teeth on Mary Ruth's wrist. She'd got hold of one of my pigtails that Gramma had fixed for me, with dark green ribbons to match my trike. And then Daddy's hands were on us, lifting all three of us at once in one motion.

We were still kicking and screaming as he lined us up against the side of Gramma's building and said, "Stay there and keep quiet."

Except for our heavy breathing, we stood still as the row of cars parked along the curb a few feet away.

"You girls can't act like this, like a pack of wild hyenas, screaming over a little trike," he continued, standing really tall, both hands on his hips. "Now listen and listen well. I'm going upstairs. And if I hear you fighting again once I get up there, I'm going to come back down and take all three of these trikes away. Do you understand?"

We all looked down at the sidewalk and nodded.

"And you two, keep your hands off Laura's trike for now," he said to Kathy and Mary Ruth. "She'll find out soon enough she's too small to ride it. Do you understand?"

They nodded their heads.

"Don't just nod like deaf mutes. Say it out loud."

"Yes, Daddy, we understand," they both said.

He turned and walked toward the door, opened it and headed up the stairs.

I wanted to prove everybody wrong. I wanted to prove that I could ride my trike as good as anybody. I marched up to the trike, put my left foot on a pedal and tried to lift my right leg up over the seat so I could get on, but instead, I fell on the sidewalk, scraping my elbow.

"See, she can't even get on. How's she gonna ride?" Mary Ruth whispered to Kathy.

"Yeah, she'll never do it," Kathy hissed back. They slid down the edge of the building and squatted on the sidewalk, arms folded over their chests, smiling as I fell again and again trying to get on.

Each fall made me more determined to find a way to ride my trike. I took a running jump and landed briefly on the seat and then fell off the other side, scraping myself up some more.

5

Kathy giggled softly at this and said, "See, she really is too puny for that trike."

"Yeah, when's she gonna give up?" Mary Ruth said.

I tried and fell again, and the trike plopped on top of me. I wiggled out from under. Then I yanked and tugged on different parts of the trike until, finally, it was right side up again. It was a little scratched on the side of the front fender, and the white seat had a big scrape on it too. I dragged it over to the tree growing in the patch of green grass between the sidewalk and the curb, leaned its rear against the trunk and climbed on from the back. And then I cracked a proud smile right there on the big white seat.

"What are you smiling at? You're not going anywhere, Laura Kapora," said Kathy.

"Yeah, you still can't pedal it, Kapoo," Mary Ruth taunted.

So I stretched and stretched until, at last, I got the trike moving by a combination of leaning forward onto the handlebars, batting my feet at the pedals and sliding back onto the seat. After I inched forward two whole sidewalk squares without falling off, I was exhausted, bleeding and bruised and ready to just ride one of the smaller trikes.

"Done now," I announced, sitting tall on the seat. Kathy and Mary Ruth rushed to the trike. Each of them grabbed a handlebar, and I slid off. They started pulling.

"You hafta ask," I said.

"What?" Kathy sneered.

"You hafta ask me. It's my trike," I insisted.

"Okay, Laura," Kathy said, with an ugly thump on the Laura like I'm a big lump in a bedspread she's trying to squish down. "Can we ride it now?"

"Yes," I said as I leaped onto one of the beat up red trikes. I watched the two of them wrestle until Kathy was on my trike and pedaling fast down the sidewalk. As I watched the green and white streamers flowing in the wind, I was mad that Kathy, Mary Ruth and Daddy were right about the trike being too big for me because I wanted to be right for once. But at least I rode my birthday trike a little bit that day, and I was the one who gave it its first scratch. I pedaled hard, chasing Kathy. Mary Ruth jumped on the other red trike and followed too. Instantly she and I became cops chasing Kathy, the robber, until Gramma called us in for lunch. Daddy and Uncle John, "Unc," were already at the table. They're always talking about one sort of project or another. Well, it's usually Daddy talking and Unc laughing along at his jokes. Unc's so quiet, you hardly notice him coming and going—the complete opposite of Daddy, and he's as plump as Daddy is tall and thin. Plus he's younger than Daddy, but some of his hair is already white, like Gramma's. Daddy's hair is all fine, shiny, and dark as night. My hair's like that too.

Unc lives here with Gramma, Daddy, Kathy, Mary Ruth and me. But I don't get to see him all that much, because when he's not at work teaching arithmetic to big kids, he's in Gramma's basement making jewelry and pottery and radios. And I don't go in the basement much. First because basements are dark and creepy and make great homes for spiders and ghosts and other scary things, and second because in Gramma's basement there's a big pile of black coal that Daddy and Unc take turns shoveling into this stove with fire inside. I'm afraid it'll just suck me up if I go near, even if the door's closed.

Daddy and Unc, they love me. But Gramma loves me more. I know this by the way we melt into each other when I climb into her lap. I lose track of where I end and she begins. Daddy and Unc lift me up high into the air sometimes. They each do it for all three of us in turn when they come in the front door. First Kathy, then Mary Ruth, and then me. I love it when it's my turn, and they spin me around. I laugh and giggle and snort. It's like I'm one of the sparrows outside soaring up, up beyond the trees. Then it's over, fast as a slap, and they're off to work, or to answer a phone call, or to fix a broken window. But Gramma with her voice so kind and hair white and fluffy is always here. It doesn't matter if I make a lot of noise, or if my sticky fingers leave dark spots on the swirling patterns of her silky smooth house dresses. My fingers, my shoes, my spit, my tears are welcome in her lap anytime.

Sometimes she feeds me right in her lap, fruit cocktail in heavy syrup, but not from the can. No, the can she opens in the kitchen with her slow moving, gnarly fingers. They're so different than mine, so lovely to touch. They have wrinkles and veins sticking up and looking like they're trying to tell me a story I can't quite understand, and long hard nails to press with my fingertips. These hands pour all the yummy chunks of pear, peach, apple and just a few cherries into a glass bowl of crystal that fits right into Gramma's palm. Then she sticks in a spoon, a "Laura-sized spoon" she says, because it's small enough for my mouth to get around without scraping my teeth. Then, ever so slowly, she walks into the living room. It's always in the living room on one of her straight-backed upholstered chairs that I climb into her lap for fruit cocktail, even though in the kitchen there's a table with a white-flecked top and shiny silver trim, legs that are cool against my fingertips, and matching chairs that I like to bounce on. We could feed me fruit cocktail there, but we don't. There's the dining room too, between the kitchen and the living room, with a lace-covered table and chairs with soft dark brown seats with faint golden stripes, and cabinets full of dishes and old stuff—antiques, Gramma calls them—like a box lined with royal blue velvet with Gramma's silver inside. That was a wedding present from long ago when she married my grampa. He went to Heaven when Daddy and Unc were boys, and he never came back. Gramma has a picture of him. He's got brown hair slicked down and a stern look in his eye. He's wearing a green suit that looks a little too tight. We could feed me fruit cocktail there too, with Grampa in his frame, keeping an eye on us, but we don't.

I have another grampa. Grampa O'Neill. He's slow moving like Gramma with a fringe of white hair around a sad, plump face. He used to hold my hand and lead me down the stairs in front of his great big house on Garfield Boulevard. It has giant round columns that hold up the roof above his front porch. There aren't any columns here on Birchwood Avenue. Grampa O'Neill never comes here. He's never sat in Gramma's living room with us where sunlight from Birchwood Avenue flows in, muted by the light layer of soot on the windows and curtains that gives everything inside a snuggly, smoky warm feel. I get plenty of sunshine outside in front, on the sidewalk. Inside I get this lap, this way of being with Gramma, where all the wonderful sounds and smells and rushing of the world stop for a while, until I'm ready to go into the bright again, which I do several times each day, happily, except for when Gramma says it's time for a nap.

I hate naps. Whenever Gramma says it's nap time I scream and cry and bounce up and down. I don't do it on purpose; it just happens like when Daddy lights a match to a cigarette, it lights up. I light up like that when anybody says it's nap time. But Gramma takes my hand and just walks me to Unc's room, me bouncing up and down all the way. She lifts me into Unc's bed saying, "There we go now." And the funny thing is before she's out of the room I'm asleep.

We don't nap under Unc's covers; we stay on top. And that's not where we sleep at night because, well, at night that's Unc's place. He gets the room all to himself. When Daddy's home he has the living room couch, and Kathy and Mary Ruth have the dining room. Gramma makes neat beds for them by putting dining room chairs together. She covers the seats with pillows to make them nice and soft, and then a sheet folded just so, so each group of chairs is like a miniature bed. Kathy and Mary Ruth climb in, and Gramma covers each of them with another folded sheet and a blanket and gives each of them a pillow for her head too. I don't know why they don't fall out, but they never do. Gramma says it's because they don't roll around as much as I do.

Each night I fall asleep in Gramma's bed. Tucked under the covers, I clutch Binkie, my pink blanket, with both hands, and lean against Gramma's soft breast. But once I'm asleep, Gramma says there's no holding me still. I tumble and roll all over the place. She says it's because I never stop being a scamp, even in my sleep. Every morning I wake up in a little cardboard box at the end of her bed that she's lined with a

soft yellow blanket to cushion my fall. I always fall off the
foot of the bed. It's just one of those things that happens sure
as the sun rides through the sky. And Gramma leans down
and says, "Good morning, Laura, you little rascal, you. In
the box again, are you?" Laughing, she reaches her hands
down, and I grab hold of her wrists. She lifts me up, puts
me onto the floor, and I slide into my day, happy to leave my
dreams behind because each night when I'm tossing around
in Gramma's bed, I'm having the same dream again and again,
and I'm glad it skitters off to wherever dreams go once I'm
on the floor in the morning light, ready to play.

It seems like my dream takes place inside of a gigantic
bubble that's floating through a midnight blue-black sky and
totally disconnected from everything. There are no stars,
and it's so cold it makes me shiver to think about it. And the
bubble, well, it's like it's been painted, maybe with a grayish
sort of paint so it's not shiny, but you can still see through it
to the vast outside nothingness. Inside the bubble are Kathy
and Mary Ruth and me. Just us. We're all dressed up in bright
peacock and fire-colored party dresses and petticoats and
pink wool coats that aren't as long as the dresses. We have
bright red circles on our cheeks sort of like Raggedy Ann
dolls. Yummy cookie crumbs cling to our fingers. There's a
sidewalk. It's a little bit cracked but not as much as the one
outside Gramma's. And there's a walk up to the front door of
a house that I know in the dream is home. Kathy and Mary
Ruth have on shiny black party shoes, but mine are sturdier,
and white. Baby shoes.

The dream always starts with me trying to catch up with
Kathy and Mary Ruth, but they're way ahead. I've just turned

off the sidewalk onto the front walk. Kathy is already at the front door to the house at the end of the walk, her hand on the knob. And Mary Ruth is behind her about to step on the bottom stair. The stairs are concrete, and there aren't many of them, not a whole flight like at Gramma's. Then Kathy turns, runs down the stairs, and says to Mary Ruth, "There's nobody home." Those words. "There's nobody home." When I hear them, it's like someone breathes all the cold air in the entire world into my body so I'm Popsicle cold inside out, and that pushes my heart up through my throat and out my mouth, and it floats off into the sky like a big red star. And while I'm feeling this, Kathy runs off calling, "I'm going 'round back to look." Then Mary Ruth turns to me and says, "There's nobody home."

I just freeze there feeling the cold breathing into me again and my heart getting pushed out again and again. It's so dark, and it feels like the sidewalk and house are spinning, and just off the walk is not solid ground with grass, but something shiny and blue that I know will swallow me up if I fall off the path. I'm stuck. I'm afraid to move, and then Mary Ruth runs up to the door and tries it herself. It doesn't open. She rushes off too, calling to me, "Going back to look," and she disappears.

I'm left there on the path feeling so alone, thinking I probably don't need to check the door since it didn't work for either of my sisters. Then I think I'll go 'round back too, but I'm scared. I can't see the backyard so I'm not sure if it's really there. My mind floods with questions. No answers. I grow more afraid and the bubble spins faster and faster. I feel numb. Then the bubble bursts. After that, I often go right back to the beginning of the dream. Sometimes I drift into a new dream. Sometimes I wake up, and it's morning. Then I'm relieved that I'm in the cozy box and Gramma is leaning over me.

Gramma makes everything bad disappear. Nothing is scary here on Birchwood Avenue.

We live on the first floor, just one set of stairs up from the sidewalk. The Flanagans are in a building just like Gramma's on one side, and Mrs. Greenman is in the same kind of building on the other side. They live on the first floor of their buildings too. So my world doesn't go up farther than that. I know people live on the upper floors, but I've never met them, and I'm not allowed to crawl up and knock on their doors. But I don't even have to knock at Mrs. Greenman's and the Flanagans'. I just climb up the stairs, put my hand on the doorknob, twist a little, push, and I'm in.

Mrs. Greenman lives alone, except for her two little dogs. They have long bodies and really short legs, and I love to stand over them because it makes me feel big for a change. One of them is solid brown, the same color as Mrs. Greenman's hair. The other is black and brown. He has brown rings around his eyes, so he looks like he's wearing a mask. The dogs have high, tinny barks. Mrs. Greenman's voice is high and tinny too, for a grown-up. But her words are splashed with lonesome, especially when she talks about her children. She shows me these papers, real thin and pretty so you can see the light from the window coming through them. They're full of lovely blue swirls that fly across the pages, like angels. She says they're letters from her daughter who lives far away. She misses her daughter. Sometimes she folds a letter very slowly making sure it's creased nice and even, and then she sticks it inside her dress at the neckline and slides it down between her sagging skin and her underwear. Then she looks out the window and pats her chest. It makes me so sad I can hardly breathe.

Mrs. Greenman always gives me a piece of chocolate just before I go. She lets me choose from what she calls an assortment—all these candies in a box each surrounded by its own pleated dark brown paper. I know there must be some good ones in her assortments, like chocolate-covered cherries or milk chocolate with caramel inside, but I always get one with this bitter kind of fruit in the middle. After one bite, I have to get outside quick so I can spit it out into the dirt.

The Flanagans' house is completely different than Mrs. Greenman's because it's full of kids like me. I go inside, and one of them will just call to their mom, "Laura's here," and she calls back, "Okay then," and I just fall in with the crowd. My favorite is jumping on their beds. I like to scribble in their coloring books too, and try to dress up dolls, which I'm not all that good at yet. If it's an especially hot day, sometimes they pack everybody up, including me, and we go visit the Lake Michigan waves. One of the biggest kids will always run to let Gramma know they've got me, and we're all heading to the beach.

I love squeezing into their sedan. There are so many of us, sometimes the bigger kids have not one, but two of us smaller kids on their laps, just stacked one on top of each other. Then there are always a couple on the floor in the front and the back squished in. When we reach the beach, we all fold out, and we run through the sand, so soft and warm, and a beautiful color. It looks like our drinks when Unc every so often, with a wink of one of his bright blue eyes, lets us have just a little bit of his coffee poured into our milk.

I like to race along the shore, hot dog in my hand, because it takes me so long to eat I can't sit still on the blanket the amount of time it would actually take to finish it. I race in and out of the waves as they lap onto the wet sand and pretend my footprints are made by an invisible child, someone who lives in the lake. I think she eats the silvery dead fish that wash up in long, narrow piles on the shore.

I don't know how to swim like some of the big Flanagan kids do, but sometimes one of the big boys will take me on his shoulders and walk out to where the water's over my head. But I'm never worried. They never even pretend to drop me. Gramma doesn't worry either. She says if I don't come around to the kitchen for a while, she knows I'm at the Flanagans'. If it gets to be time for my nap, she sends Kathy or Mary Ruth to fetch me, and I come right back.

All in all, life is really grand here on Birchwood Avenue. Grand is one of Gramma's favorite words. When she's really pleased with something, she says, "Oh, my, my, isn't that grand!" And that's how I feel just about every day. There are so many new things happening, and not too many fights with Kathy or Mary Ruth, and not too many spankings from Daddy or Unc for doing things I don't know are wrong until I do them. I wouldn't want to trade places with anyone, ever.

But yesterday Daddy scooped up Kathy and Mary Ruth and took them and their red suitcases away. I thought he might be taking them back to Mantino, and I'm glad I was wrong.

Kathy and Mary Ruth got stuck there for a while, and I

visited them there with Uncle Dean. He's one of the O'Neills. I think I was living with the O'Neills then, but my memories are like little scraps of paper I find on the floor sometimes. Whatever bigger pieces they came from are long gone. I do remember Aunt Ruth taking Kathy and Mary Ruth for a ride one day. She's an O'Neill too. She came back, but they didn't.

After that it felt like my soul just leaked out through my shoes. I was floating along with no particular thoughts, no wants, no ideas. Just empty. And I stopped talking. Not on purpose. I still made noise, but without Kathy and Mary Ruth listening to me, I just couldn't make word sounds anymore. Funny thing is that nobody seemed to notice. Different people took turns lifting me from one place to another like a figurine that needs to be moved so you can dust a shelf. I didn't care where they put me. One spot was the same as another. Grampa O'Neill came and went from his office downstairs where he helps sick people get better. Way up in one of the bedrooms where I never went was Gramma O'Neill. She's always in bed because her heart is bad. I had to be really quiet around her bad heart. She scares me so much that I forget she's my gramma too.

Then one day Uncle Dean and I were riding in his car. Snow fell outside on the windshield and the wipers went back and forth, back and forth, making a strange wheezing, scraping sound over and over. We traveled for a long time, neither one of us making a sound. Then we stopped in front of the biggest, darkest building I'd ever seen. Just seeing it there like a dungeon above ground behind the snow flurries made me sad. I don't know why. Uncle Dean's shoes left footprints in the light layer of snow behind us as he carried me to the porch. "This is Mantino, and we're here to visit your sisters," he said as he rang the bell. A nun opened the door and led us into a little room just off the entryway.

Uncle Dean got all stiff and quiet as he put me down on the floor. It seems all the grown-ups in my family get that way whenever a priest or nun is around, which is pretty often because we've got a bunch of them in our family. You never know when one of them is going to pop in and land on the sofa and change everything for a while. I'm not sure that they're real people though, covered in all that black. I don't think they have bodies like everybody else. Another nun walked up to us. Uncle Dean called her Mother Superior. He acted like maybe Mother Superior had Daddy's belt behind her back and any minute might take a whack at him.

Then through the doorway, heading into the room came another nun, with Kathy and Mary Ruth in tow. I ran up to them. I expected them to run up to me, but the nun kept hold of them really tight. I had part of a dog biscuit in the pocket of my coat, and I held it out to them. I had until that moment forgotten how much I like to nibble on dog biscuits. They peered at it really close and smiled. I wondered if they liked dog biscuits too and if they knew where the ones in my pocket came from.

"Say hello to your sisters, Laura," Uncle Dean said.

I nodded to them, since my voice wasn't working. The nun holding on to them let go, and we crowded together there on the floor to examine my stash of biscuit chunks. But then Mother Superior took a glass bell with tiny flowers painted on it from deep within her black robes and shook it to make it jingle. Then she said, "Come on, girls, it's time for lunch."

I couldn't believe it. We hadn't even decided what game to play, let alone play one. We went down the hall to another room. It had two long tables, and there were kids already sitting at them. None of them was smiling. They weren't even moving. And they were all pale, like the faded curtains in Gramma's kitchen. That's how these kids were, except for their eyes. They flashed hard and mean right at me. I'd never seen kids like them before, and I wondered if maybe, like the nuns, they might not be real.

Uncle Dean sat me on top of three phone books piled on a chair so I could reach the table. A chubby nun with a rosy face came through a swinging door. She pushed soup bowls on a wobbly cart, and she put them down, one at each place. Kathy and Mary Ruth were across the table from me, and they weren't sitting together. I wondered why we were sitting all split up. Then Mother Superior led us in saying grace. I bowed my head and listened.

After the "Amen" Mary Ruth said, "I want Laura by me."

Mother Superior tapped her napkin to her lips and frowned. "Now, Mary Ruth, remember your manners. Sit down and eat quietly," she said.

But Mary Ruth said, "I want Laura. I haven't seen her in so long. Why can't we play?"

Mother Superior raised her voice, "Mary Ruth, we've talked about how important it is to behave appropriately. You have to learn to get along like everyone else."

Mary Ruth didn't give up. "She's my sister. Mine!"

"Stop fussing, Mary Ruth! What makes you think you deserve special treatment?" Mother Superior hissed.

I'd never heard anyone talk to Mary Ruth like that. She wasn't just mad like Daddy gets sometimes. Something in her voice and the look in her eyes was saying she didn't like Mary Ruth at all. I wanted Uncle Dean to stand up and do something, but he just sat there next to me and said, "There now, Mary Ruth, do what Mother Superior says."

Mary Ruth started to cry, and Mother Superior said, "Stop crying, Mary Ruth. Only babies cry. You must behave like a young lady."

But Mary Ruth started wailing and screaming. So Mother Superior motioned to the soup nun, and the soup nun grabbed Mary Ruth by the arm, pulled her from her chair, and yanked her to a door that led to a dark hallway.

Mary Ruth screamed, "Lemme go, lemme go!"

The kitchen nun slapped her with a big loud WHAP across the face and dragged her out of the room. Mary Ruth was still screaming, "Lemme go, lemme go! I wanna see my sister. I wanna see my sister."

Slurps, conversations, coughs, sniggers, the weight of bodies shifting in chairs. Everything stopped. All was quiet. We all listened as Mary Ruth's screams got softer and softer until they faded out entirely. I looked up at Uncle Dean and he said, "Don't you start crying too, Laura. Just be good and eat your soup."

I didn't want to eat my soup. I wasn't even hungry when Uncle Dean plunked me down at the table. And the soup looked like dishwater with a few slices of celery floating on top.

Mother Superior fixed her gaze on me. Then she turned to Uncle Dean and said, "Finicky, isn't she?"

He fiddled a little bit with his necktie and said, "Oh, now, I don't think—"

Mother Superior interrupted, "Well, don't worry. She'll get over that in short order once she joins her sisters here."

I sat there staring at the soup forever, glancing over at Kathy every so often. She was glancing at me too, but it seemed each time I looked she was paler, blending in more and more with the other kids. And then Mother Superior rang her bell and said, "Okay children. Line up." Without a peep, they formed two perfect rows. Kathy gave me one last look as she took her place in line. And they filed out the door. Uncle Dean picked me up, said his good-byes to Mother Superior, and carried me outside.

On the sidewalk the snow that had held Uncle Dean's footsteps was gone. He carried me to a playground area under the dark shadow of Mantino and put me in a swing, locking me in with the little wooden bar that slides down. He pushed me. Back and forth I went. I felt like I was disappearing, that I was getting buried in the freezing air, and I didn't care. I went limp in the swing, with the world spinning around me. I wished I could just spin off to a place where everything was warm, a place where Mantino could not trap little kids and turn them pale, unhappy and mean. I wanted a place where I could play with my sisters all afternoon.

The next time I was in the car with Uncle Dean I thought we were going back to Mantino. My suitcase was packed. I thought he'd be leaving me there, and I'd have to start living on dishwater soup. Then we pulled up in front of Gramma's building. And that was it. The day my real life began. Uncle Dean stayed in the hall and put my suitcase just inside the door. I walked into the living room. Then he turned and left. No good-bye.

And then Gramma said my name that wonderful way only she does. I ran to her and she lifted me up. She looked to the parlor and cried out, "Look, Kathy, Mary Ruth, Laura's here. Isn't that grand?" Kathy and Mary Ruth looked up from a puzzle they had spread out on the floor. They didn't smile. They were different, like they had a halo around them, but it wasn't a bright angel's halo. It was dark. It was a Mantino halo, beaming mean all over them. "Oh," Kathy said, and looked back down at the puzzle. Mary Ruth did the same.

I followed Gramma to the kitchen where she opened the first can of fruit cocktail I'd ever seen.

"You're going to love this, Laura, especially the cherries, don't you think so?" she asked. I didn't answer. She went on as though I had.

"Although, the pears are awfully nice. You like pears, don't you?" I still didn't answer. I would have if I could have.

She talked to me the whole way to the kitchen and back, asking questions as though she expected any second I was going to answer. In the living room she sat me on her lap and urged me to savor each little piece of fruit, paying no mind that I was silent. This went on day after day. She sat me on her lap and talked to me while she fed me soft-boiled egg in the morning, bits of bologna sandwich at lunch, orange peanut-shaped candy in the afternoons, until one morning she asked me, "How many eggs do you want for breakfast, Laura, one or two?"

I said, "Two."

"Two eggs it is then," she replied.

That was it. I've been talking ever since.

Now my sparkly red suitcase is packed again and sitting by the door. Gramma and I are going on our ride. We're having an adventure. The sun's warming me top to bottom. We're all dressed up—white gloves, white hat for her, white ribbons for me. She took extra care with my hair this morning, brushing it soft and slow. She says pretty soon my hair will be long enough for a ponytail. I can't wait for that. I've got white patent leather shoes, too, with straps I can buckle myself, and anklets with scalloped lace folded over looking oh so pretty. Gramma's shoes are black boots that lace up way past her ankles. It takes her a long time to get the laces just so around each little hook. They're the only shoes she ever wears out of the house. Inside she's in floppy slippers that scrape lightly on the floor when she walks. I'm wearing a white dress with little bows of all different colors on it. Kathy and Mary Ruth each have one of these dresses too. Gramma says that Mommy got them for us and that Mommy used to dress us real nice. Gramma's dress has a white lace collar, like my socks, and lace at the end of her sleeves. It's full of lots of different colored flowers, like my different-colored bows. We're as matching as we can possibly be. I'm ready for an adventure. Gramma says today we're going to meet my mother and that Kathy and Mary Ruth are already there.

The doorbell rings. "Time to go, honey," Gramma says. She grabs her purse and my suitcase. And we're off. The cab is like a car. But there's so much room inside it makes me giddy. There are even two little seats you can pull up from the floor to make room for more people. I think I've ridden in something like this before. It was big and shiny and black with seats just like these that pull up, but I can't remember when it was. Now I wish Kathy and Mary Ruth were here too in this grand cab with Gramma. We could have a tea party and look out the windows as Chicago's sidewalks and buildings fly by.

Even though we have lots of room to spread out in, Gramma and I are snuggled together. She is holding my hands in her hands, like hers are the bread and mine are the peanut butter in a sandwich. Every so often she lifts the one on top and just pats my hands a couple times, ever so gently. Holding hands with Gramma is one of my absolute favorite things, and holding hands with Gramma, in a cab, on a sunny day, on the way to see my mother has to be what Heaven is like.

I have a little smile growing from deep inside me. It's been so long since I've seen Mommy that as far as I'm concerned everything that isn't right between us doesn't matter. Seeing her, being in the same room with her, even if she doesn't want to talk to me, or hold me, or even look at me, that'll be okay now. I'll stay near her on the floor, playing with my toy that makes sparks with a little circle that goes around and around. I'll be quiet and wait for her to come to me. When she does, I'll be sure to smile. I will be happy with anything she does; she doesn't have to be my pal like Gramma.

It didn't used to be okay with me, the way Mommy ignores me, and especially the way she just goes away sometimes with no explanation. People think because I'm so small and don't talk that well, or all the much, that I don't understand what they're saying. But I do understand a lot, and if I don't understand something the grown-ups say, I keep all their words inside. It's like I'm a storage box that's also a puzzle, and each day I pick up new words and put them in and shake things up, and I remember things, and I think things over and figure a lot of stuff out. It's one of my favorite things to do, figure things out on my own while I'm playing with crayons, or petting Mrs. Greenman's dogs, or chewing one of Gramma's fresh-baked biscuits. I'm always thinking and figuring things out. That's my secret, and I've been trying to figure out what's happened to Mommy. There haven't been many clues.

One time I was alone out front at Gramma's. I was licking a Popsicle and playing with a doll buggy. Kathy and Mary Ruth came down and told me that Mommy was upstairs visiting and they'd gotten to say hi to her.

I thought that if they got to say hi, I ought to be able to say hi too, so I put the Popsicle in the buggy, and began the long climb up the stairs. It seemed long anyway. I was so much smaller then. I crawled up; I couldn't walk up them back then. When I reached the top the door was already open. I stood up and charged into the living room. And there they were, my wonderful Mommy and Daddy at the edge of the living room by the parlor up near a lace-covered window. They faced each other, holding hands. Mommy was dressed all in pink. Pink hat, pink suit, pink purse, even pink shoes. I saw her there looking like Gramma's cameo, only in full color. She was absolutely beautiful, like a princess. I was about to run across into the room when Daddy turned his head to glare at me and said sternly, "Go away, Laura. Your mother can't see you now."

I did manage to stop myself after a step or two, but then I stood there gaping at them. His words just didn't fit my idea of what was supposed to happen. I couldn't believe Mommy didn't want to see me. I was hoping she'd look over at me, smile, and say something, at least hi. But she kept looking straight ahead at Daddy as though I wasn't there at all. Then Daddy said, raising his voice some, "You heard me, Laura. Your mother can't see you now. She's on her way to church. Now scram."

I still couldn't move. I was taking that in, the fact that Mommy was on her way to church. I was wondering why she wouldn't even turn her head to say hi before she left.

Then Daddy said, "I'm warning you."

He took a step in my direction. I knew I'd better go before he took another step if I didn't want to get whacked all the way to Mrs. Greenman's. So I turned, went out the door, and started to crawl down. I felt so jumbled up. I didn't know what to think. I hoped Mommy would come after me. I moved extra slow to give her a chance to catch up. But with each step down, feeling the rubbed, worn hall carpet on my hands I felt worse and worse. By the time I got back outside with Kathy and Mary Ruth, my Popsicle was just a puddle with a stick on top. I flopped down on the sidewalk.

Kathy and Mary Ruth both asked, "Did you see Mommy? And I replied, "Yup."

I got up, took the handle of my buggy and started pushing it back and forth on the sidewalk.

"Daddy told Gramma that Mommy's back at home. But we can't go. Mommy needs to be by herself for a while before we go back," said Kathy.

"Wouldn't wanna be by myself," Mary Ruth said.

I decided then and there that I wasn't going to like Mommy if she didn't like me back. Not too long after that, Mommy came with Aunt Ruth to pick Kathy and Mary Ruth and me up and take us home. Mommy didn't even get out of the car. It was Aunt Ruth who rang Gramma's bell to fetch us. She looked especially beautiful with her long red hair tickling her shoulders and not one wrinkle in her robin's-egg blue dress and not one scuff on her matching shoes. She stood so much taller than my Gramma and so much straighter. I clung to Gramma's hand harder than I ever had the whole way down the stairs. When I saw Mommy just staring straight ahead, looking a lot like she did when she was facing Daddy the other day, only this time dressed in a gray dress with white trim, something snapped. I started jumping up and down and screaming, having a real conniption fit. They had to struggle to stuff me into the back seat with Kathy and Mary Ruth.

I watched Aunt Ruth walk around the car and get into the driver's seat. I was sniffling, but not screaming anymore. Before she started the engine she turned her lovely head around, leaned as far as possible into the back seat and said, "You're a very, very bad girl for treating your mother this way, Laura. You should be ashamed of yourself." Mommy just kept staring straight ahead out the front window.

Well, that shut me up. I didn't know I'd been treating my mother any way at all, but at that moment I felt badness just creeping through me. Kathy and Mary Ruth shrank away from me as if this badness was something they could catch. I can't remember a thing about the rest of the ride or if we ever made it home.

But what do I care about that now? Birds are chirping happily, and I see all kinds of flowers blooming in the yards we're passing. It's a grand day! Gramma and I are quiet, still holding hands as the cab turns down this beautiful street with big trees on each side, leaning toward each other like they're trying to kiss over the cars below. It's so much quieter than the bigger street we turned off.

"Pretty," I say to Gramma.

"Yes, it is, Laura. It's Richmond Street," Gramma replies.

The cab stops in front of a little gray house. "This is it," Gramma says.

The driver opens the door for us, and then helps Gramma up the front stairs, holding her by the elbow. Then he pats me on the head saying, "Good luck, little one."

I'm certain I've never been to this house before, but then Daddy opens the door and says, "Welcome home, Laura."

Gramma and I step inside to a space too small to be a room, but not long enough to be a hall. There's a table about as tall as I am with a vase full of pink carnations in front of me. To the right is a doorway to the living room. Daddy steps through and walks across the room, and stands by a smiling woman leaning against the door to another room. By the window on a couch are Kathy, Mary Ruth and a hunched up man with thin, dark hair and yellowy gray skin. To his right is a big curvy piece of furniture with a bench in front of it. And under that is the most beautiful dog, with long white, black and brown hair. Daddy calls me over. I slip away from Gramma and walk across the room. Daddy is holding the woman's arm, and he says, "Laura, this is your mother. Say hello."

She smiles looking me right in the face and leans down a little toward me and says, "Hello, Laura." I'm feeling really strange because there is my own mother standing in front of me and I don't recognize her.

Lots of things flood into my mind all at once. One thing I know for sure is that Daddy is always right, and if he says this is my mother, she must be. And I think about things changing, like if I put biscuit dough into my mouth and chew, it disappears. It doesn't exist anymore. If Gramma takes some dough and puts it into the oven, when she takes it out, it's fluffy and crusty and golden brown. If I put some dough in a bowl of water, it gets bigger and starts to sort of melt, and the water starts to look like milk. Other things change too, like my trike was shiny, and now it's dull and full of rust. And Kathy, Mary Ruth and I are always changing. Mary Ruth's hair is darker now than Kathy's, and just a bit ago their hair was the same color. We're always growing too. I think Mommy must have changed somehow like this.

Daddy clears his throat in irritation and says, "Say hello to your mother, Laura."

"Hello," I say staring into a face that has sharp, little brown eyes. It's not like I can say for sure how she's different. I don't exactly remember Mommy's eyes because I can't remember looking into them, but I don't think they used to be brown.

"Go sit on the couch now next to Grampa Adams," Daddy says.

I look at the man. He looks so sour, like a pickle. I think of my grampa who just looks out from his picture frame at Gramma's. And I think of Grampa O'Neill. I haven't thought of him in a while. I look over at Mommy and wonder if maybe this Grampa Adams is really a changed Grampa O'Neill, but Daddy didn't say he's Grampa O'Neill, so I think he must be someone different. I sure hope he is.

I sit down next to Grampa Adams. I'm not the least bit inclined to lean into him like I remember leaning into Grampa O'Neill. Grampa Adams is looking at me like I'm a mosquito about to land on him. Then the dog under the curvy thing growls.

"That's Rusty, Laura, Grampa Adams' dog," Daddy says.

Grampa Adams says, "You aah ehh better stay away from ehh him. He no like aah childaren."

The way Grampa Adams talks, he says the same words, but they're all different sounding. I have to listen hard because he stops and starts at different times than I'm used to.

I don't ask about how Mommy got to be so different, where she was when she was gone or where Grampa Adams came from. This is all just more stuff to figure out, and I'm pretty good at that. I'm thinking all of this over, thinking maybe Gramma will come in and sit next to me, and I'll be more comfortable, but then Daddy says to Gramma, "Well, it's time to get you on home now, Mom."

Gramma hasn't even stepped into the room. I didn't think that meeting Mommy would mean saying goodbye to Gramma, especially this way, without Gramma even coming into the room and having a piece of candy or something. Gramma didn't tell me she was going to leave me here. How can she have ridden so happily all that way with me and known she was just going to slip away? I slide off the couch and take a few steps toward Gramma, thinking if Gramma's going I'm going too, but Daddy says, "Get back on the couch, Laura. You're staying here with your family where you belong."

So I go back to the couch, hoping Gramma will say something to make Daddy change his mind. "Goodbye, my sweet girls," Gramma says to Kathy, Mary Ruth and me, blowing each of us a kiss with trembling lips and wobbly hand. Then Daddy takes her by the elbow, and they go out of the door.

I almost cry right there on the couch, but I remember how Aunt Ruth said that day when she and Mommy came to pick us up that I was bad for not wanting to leave Gramma and go away with Mommy. I don't want to be bad, so I hold my breath and keep quiet. I feel tears come into my eyes. I scrunch up my face and squeeze the tears out and brush them away with my fingertips. I wipe them off on the bright bow pattern of my dress, and Mommy doesn't notice, thank goodness.

Hank didn't shed one tear when my body was lowered into the ground. He laughed. Oh how he laughed. Guffaws and chortles and gasps came bubbling up, a whirlpool on overdrive. He sucked in his breath, tried to control the force bursting from his core, but he could not. Nor could he feel my hand on his shoulder, telling him everything would work out; he doubted whether I ever really loved him, wished he had fallen for some other girl. And he laughed. Even under sedation, he laughed on and on. It wasn't until he realized our girls were slipping away from him and might be split up forever, each to a different home, that the storm finally receded. He rose from the detritus of our love, reinforced. He gathered his children, locked all memories of me and all notions of romantic love in a cold, hard part of his soul and moved on.

Mary Agnes

Richmond Street

I love Chicago. There are so many reasons why. I didn't know when we moved to Richmond Street that our house, Gramma's building and Grampa O'Neill's home are all really part of the same place. But they are. Knowing that makes them all connected, like Chicago's one giant house, and when I've gone from Garfield Boulevard to Birchwood Avenue to Richmond Street, I haven't gone away so much as moved from one room to another.

I love that Chicago goes on and on and on, block after block after block. I think about how fine our little block is. We go along, Daddy driving Kaisery, our pink Kaiser, Daddy's favorite brand of car. Most days Kaisery is busy speeding Daddy to work or off to a far-away place called Hinsdale where he and Unc are building us a new house. But on just about every Sunday, Kaisery carries us all to Gramma's. There and back again we'll go on forever down wide streets, full of traffic lights, and buses, and cars, and trucks honking their horns, and people rushing along the sidewalks. This is exciting. But then Daddy turns Kaisery onto Richmond Street. It's like a different world, so quiet and peaceful and pretty, like a butterfly on a branch. It's got to be the best block there is.

Sometimes I think of all the other blocks as Kaisery zooms along, and I get so amazed thinking that each one is full of people, people I don't know, but people like us opening their doors each morning and going out and maybe thinking their block is the best block in the world too. And the thought of that keeps me happy for quite a long time. In Chicago I'm part of something, something big, like a box of corn flakes. And the box is grand, but each little flake is yummy all by itself.

We're heading to visit our new house now. It takes a long, long time to get there and back again. One of these days we'll go there and not come back. We're leaving Chicago for good, and my beautiful Richmond Street. That makes me sad.

You can't help but notice the trees on Richmond Street when you round the corner, the way the two rows arch over the street. I spend a good part of each day on the sidewalk under those trees. Sometimes I play with Kathy and Mary Ruth. But I play more often with Charlie. He lives three doors down, and he never bosses me around like they do. Each day, if I'm not outside already, he comes to the door. If I'm done with my buttermilk, I get to go right out and meet him. But if I'm not done yet, he has to wait on the porch until I've chugged the slimy stuff down.

I can't believe it's okay with Mommy for Charlie to like me, like me special, I mean. She calls us the Richmond Street sweethearts to anybody who'll listen. Charlie's just my age and just my size, and we seem to belong together like a worn pair of shoes, even though we're opposite in some ways—like he's a boy, and I'm a girl, and he's got blond hair, and mine is almost black. But I still don't know why it's okay with Mommy for him to like me so much. She says it's not right for anybody to favor any one of us over the others. She says that Gramma favored me when we lived with her, and it was oh so very wrong.

"You'll never catch me doin' what that poor old woman did, favorin' Laura the way she did. All three of the girls, they're the same to me. I don't put any one above the other," she says.

Sometimes Mommy talks like that when she's supervising our chores. She arches her plucked black eyebrows and wrinkles up her mouth in a way that makes it look like she has whiskers, so she looks like a frizzy haired cat. Then she smiles like she's about to devour a pound of pure chocolate and starts ranting half to Kathy, Mary Ruth and me, and half to the air. She pounds the same things into us day after day.

She says Kathy's the artist in the family. Mary Ruth is the smart one, and I'm the pretty one. No matter what Mary Ruth and I do, we'll never have Kathy's talent. No matter what Kathy and I do we'll never match Mary Ruth in brains, and no matter how hard they try, Kathy and Mary Ruth will never be as nice to look at as me. That's how the world is when it comes to our good points.

When it comes to our bad points, I'm always the sneak and the dunce because I make mistakes like dropping dishes and breaking them and throwing the pieces in the garbage without telling her. Kathy's always putting on airs, sighing and tilting her head like a movie star, and Mary Ruth is always a smart alec because she asks questions about stuff Mommy decides, and then she up and disagrees, knowing she'll get walloped for it later. Mommy says we're all selfish too—so selfish that we never appreciated what Gramma went through caring for us, how much trouble we all were. So on that score in terms of being selfish I guess we all are the same to her.

I never thought we caused Gramma trouble. I thought she liked being with us, and if she favored me, I guess that isn't right, but how can something that felt so wonderful be so bad? But Mommy says it was exactly that and that I'd better watch myself around Gramma. "I've got my eye on you," she says.

I'm happy I still get to see Gramma on the weekends when we all pile into Kaisery. Kathy, Mary Ruth and I race to the car, partly out of happiness that we're heading off to Gramma's, and partly so as not to be the last one inside because the last one has to sit in the middle. We're not allowed to push and shove each other either because if one of us gives another of us a push, the other one pushes back harder. Then they usually trip the third one who's starting to move past them because they're distracted. Pretty soon all three of us are rolling in the grass by the car door in one big messy pile of anger. The last time we did that, Daddy got so upset he spanked us all and sent us to bed. He and Mommy went off to Gramma's without us.

After they left, Grampa Adams came into our bedroom and lectured us about how horrid we are. I just wanted to shrink like Alice in Wonderland, or at least crawl under my bed, but as soon as one of us made the least little wiggle, he snapped at us, telling us to be still. It lasted so long I was amazed that I could actually be still for it. I'd never done it before. Finally, with our six tired eyes staring up at him,

Grampa Adams backed to the door of our room. "Why ehh bother," he said, "You ahh not worth ehh trouble." And he left. His words stuck around though. There's that saying "Sticks and stones can break my bones, but words can never hurt me." But it seems to me that words can hurt a lot. They can go somewhere inside and stay there just like a sliver.

I love going to visit Gramma even though it's not the same as it used to be. I still love her as much as ever. The trouble is even if Mommy's not actually sitting or standing between us, she's there between us just the same. Mommy says a girl is supposed to love her grandparents, but she's supposed to love her parents most of all.

So when we arrive now at Gramma's, I don't run right up to Gramma. Mommy says when I do that I'm being very selfish, and I have to think of others. So I sit next to Mary Ruth and Kathy on the couch. Mommy sits next to Gramma, each of them in one of Gramma's straight-backed chairs. Sometimes Daddy stays in the room too. Sometimes he goes into another room with Unc. Sometimes he and Unc go all the way out to work on the house in Hinsdale, where we're headed now. Sometimes they bring our cousin George along. George is almost all grown up, and his daddy is in Heaven, so Daddy and Unc are filling in for him until he gets back. After we're settled in, Mommy tells Gramma what we've been up to. Since I turned five, I got to start playing piano. That's what the giant, curvy piece of furniture in our living room is, a baby grand piano. Mommy gives Gramma updates on my progress.

She's especially happy to tell Gramma how Kathy and Mary Ruth are doing in school because it's such good news.

Our school, Darwin School, has half years, and starting in first grade kids can skip half a year at a time. Mary Ruth just skipped the second half of first grade. Kathy did that last year, and then she skipped the second half of second grade too. That makes her a whole year ahead.

Mommy's always sure to tell Gramma after she reports on their progress, "I doubt that Laura will be skipping any grades when the time comes."

"Oh, Helen, you just never know," Gramma replies.

Things are also different now at Gramma's because we can't go in and out whenever we want to. We go out when Mommy says it's okay to go, and we come in when she calls us in. We're not allowed to visit Mrs. Greenman and the Flanagans anymore either. Mommy says we barged in uninvited too many times, so we wore out our welcome.

It's the same at home on Richmond Street. We come and go only when Mommy says it's okay, and we're not supposed to ask to go out. We're just supposed to smile and get moving fast whenever she orders us outside. She says we'd break the doors down with our constant coming and going if she left it up to us. So once we're out, we're out for a long time. We're never allowed to go into the neighbors' houses either. Where we belong is at home. That's it.

I like it when we're all sitting around Gramma's dining room table. She has a lace tablecloth that she crocheted a long, long time ago. And she uses blue and white china dishes with designs so beautiful that they keep me absorbed through many dull grown-up conversations. Sometimes we have chicken, and sometimes fish and chips from this shop nearby. I usually hate fish. Whenever we pass a fish market

I gag so hard I practically throw up. But I like the fish and chips from the place near Gramma's.

After we eat, and Kathy, Mary Ruth and I wash and dry the dishes, we all stay inside for a while. It's during these after-meal times that I usually get to be right up next to Gramma. We just quietly come together for a while, and she pats my hand. I spin her wedding ring on her finger. It's always there because it couldn't slip over her swollen knuckle even if she wanted it to. For those few moments, things are just like they used to be with her and me.

Pretty soon the sky starts to get dark, Gramma shuffles around her apartment putting lights on one by one, and then it's time for us to head on home. It's always hard to leave, especially if I'm holding Gramma's hand. But once we're told it's time to go, we have to get right up and move toward the door. If it's winter, we'll put on our coats and hats and boots and scarves. Then out the door we go, down the steps, and out to Kaisery. When we're settled into the back seat, we look up to Gramma's front parlor window. And there she is standing by a dimly glowing table lamp, smiling at us and waving. We wave back. And we keep it up, all three of us and Gramma, waving back and forth, as Daddy starts up Kaisery, edges the car out of its parking space, and heads down the block and around the corner. We never stop waving until Gramma is completely out of sight.

I found out that Kathy, Mary Ruth and I were all born 14 months apart. This means there's the same amount of space between Mary Ruth and me as there is between Kathy and Mary Ruth. It doesn't seem that way. It seems that we've always been like a train where Kathy and Mary Ruth take turns being the engine and the middle car. I'm always the caboose bringing up the rear. Daddy says when it was time for Kathy to get potty trained, Mary Ruth watched and didn't want to be left out, so she potty trained herself at the same time. He also says I'm the baby of the family, and Mary Ruth had her chance to be the baby, but she blew it and let me be born. Now, he says, she's busy trying to get past Kathy so she can be the oldest. He says all this with a big smile on his face, and I think maybe he's joking, but I'm not sure.

Mommy says she thinks there's a gap between Mary Ruth and me because I've fallen on my head so many times it's made me slightly retarded. I sure hope that's not true. Mommy says this with a smile too, but I know she's not joking because it's her cat smile. I forget about all of this when I'm with Charlie though.

I step outside in the morning and there we stand side by side, Charlie and me, not knowing yet what the day holds in store. Sometimes we'll find caterpillars making their way along leaves in the bushes. Sometimes we'll see old Mrs. Piccolo wrapped in a crocheted shawl sitting in a rocking chair on her front porch. She's more wrinkled than Grampa Adams. Daddy says she smokes a corncob pipe. Sometimes we'll pop into the little store on our block. To get a good look at the candy you have to go down a few steps and pass men with big stomachs and thick cigars sticking out of their mouths like smoking brown tongues. Charlie and I never have money to buy candy, but we like to look at it once a day.

One time Charlie's grampa took both of us to a park. Charlie lives with his mommy, his grampa and his gramma. His mommy leaves early each day because she works like

Daddy does. So his gramma and grampa are in charge of him when she's gone. The day at the park with Charlie and his grampa—oh, I hope I never forget it! We walked in the warm breeze, trees and grass all around us, everything bright green. Then we came to a bridge that went over some sparkling, deep water that had white flowers floating right in it. It was magic through and through. We leaned over the wall of the bridge for a long time just looking at them so beautiful floating there. Charlie's grampa said they were water lilies. I never knew flowers could live in water before that day.

Just seeing that would have been enough. But then we went to a building his grampa said is a lodge. And in the hallway of that lodge was a bear, a huge black bear, standing up taller than Charlie's grampa. I pulled back a little bit, not sure it was safe to go up to a bear, but Charlie's grampa said it was okay. So we walked right up to it, and Charlie and I each patted the bear's legs with our hands.

Then his grampa pulled out a nickel from his pocket, put it into a slot in the bear, and it growled real loud and shook its body and moved its front paws back and forth. Charlie and I leaped away, frightened that the bear was going to lunge at us.

But his grampa said, "Don't worry. This bear would never hurt two good kids like you."

Then he gave each of us a nickel so we could have a turn at making the bear growl and move. It was so much fun I thought I might just float away, like the fuzzy white head of a big old dandelion. My head felt so light. Then his grampa had some sort of business to do in the lodge, and Charlie and I waited peacefully by the bear, every so often touching it and marveling at how a little nickel could make a big bear come alive. When he returned, we walked out of the lodge, and we got to walk over the bridge again. He let us linger a long time memorizing the water lilies. What a day that was!

Daddy took Kathy, Mary Ruth and me on a special trip too one day. We went all the way to a place called the Museum of Science and Industry. Daddy loves that place because he's a chemical engineer and that has to do with science. He loves chemicals, and he's always talking about them. Sometimes Kathy, Mary Ruth and I dance around the house to the rhythm of their names and we make up little stories: Acetylsalicylic acid went to the zoo, and hydrochloric acid went along too. What do you think the two of them would do? I don't know, oh boo hoo! Sulfuric acid ate my pants, so I threw him out onto the ants. The ants were not happy fiddledeedee. I'd better go and climb a tree.

I don't remember anything about chemicals from our visit to the museum though. What I remember is going down, down into a dark coal mine, just like the ones that grew the coal that went to Gramma's basement furnace, only smaller. Gramma doesn't get coal delivered anymore. She has a gas heater now. Mommy says, "It's about time. She must have been the last person in Chicago to switch to gas!"

Another thing at the Museum of Science and Industry that I loved was an enormous dollhouse. It is bigger than the bedroom that Kathy, Mary Ruth and I share. I swear it is. You could walk all the way around it and see perfect furniture and pictures made for each room. There was a round table in the dining room that Daddy said was modeled after a real famous table that knights used to sit at a long, long time ago. There was a rug in the shape of a bear too, a white bear. I think it would be scary to have a rug like that. I could see the bear's teeth. There was a piano in one room too. I imagined all of us gathered around Mommy playing one of her concertos in there. Looking at the rooms I felt like I was passing through a fairy tale. Mary Ruth said it used to belong to a very rich girl, but she grew up and didn't need it anymore.

Kathy, Mary Ruth and I don't have a dollhouse; we don't even own any dolls. We had a few when we first moved to Richmond Street, but one day out on the back porch, we had them undressed, and sort of twisted up. We were doctors, and they'd been hurt bad in a big car accident. We had to help. We were all three leaning over them doing a big important operation when Mommy came in and went off like a police siren, "Stop it. Stop it right now. Taking your dolls' clothes off and contorting them like that? What filth! Filthy, filthy, filth. I knew it. I knew you were dirty-minded. We'll put an end to that alrighty."

Kathy tried to explain. Kathy always goes first with this trying to explain business, her being the oldest and all, which I really appreciate because at times like this, my mind goes completely clear of thoughts and my voice just takes a vacation.

So Kathy said, "We're just playing doctor, like Grampa O'Neill. We're going to make them all better like he does with his patients."

But Mommy wouldn't hear it. "Give me those dolls this instant," she said. "That's it for you, girls. No more dolls. You're perverted. Disgusting and perverted."

She meant it too about the dolls. There hasn't been one doll in our house since that day. But I don't mind too much. I don't think Kathy and Mary Ruth mind either. I don't really know what you're supposed to do with dolls besides play doctor with them. One good thing about the doll thing is that Mommy hasn't talked about it again. Usually, if we do something wrong, it doesn't go away as easily as the dolls did.

A couple of years ago Mommy gave Kathy a dollar bill and sent her to the little store on our block to get some milk. Off she went, strutting tall down the sidewalk. A little while later she returned. Tears streamed down her cheeks, like the first drops down our windowpanes at the start of a storm.

"Where's the milk, Katherine?" Mommy asked.

"I couldn't get it."

"Why is that, Katherine?"

"I lost the dollar."

"What do you mean you lost the dollar?"

"I put it in my pocket, and when I got to the store it wasn't there."

"Oh, that's just dandy. You were walking along and it just flew out of your pocket. You expect me to believe that whopper? That's just great. It just flew out of your pocket. As if dollar bills can fly, all by themselves. I don't see any bills flying around here, but put one in your hand and it gets wings. Ha! That's what I get for trying to give a no account prima donna like you a little bit of responsibility."

"I didn't mean to lose it," Kathy said. "I'm really sorry."

"That doesn't bring the dollar back, does it. It just flew out of your pocket! Wait until your father hears about this."

That was a bad sign because when she says, "Wait until your father hears about this," it usually means one of us is going to get belted that night. We get belted for the things that make Mommy and Daddy the angriest. First we get scolded, then we maybe get slapped in the face or socked in the arm. If it's during the day and we've done something really bad, Mommy spanks us with one of those wooden paddles leftover from the toys with the rubber string and red ball on the end. She saves them all for paddling after the rubber strings break. One time the paddle broke when she was pounding on Mary Ruth. Mary Ruth laughed. That got Mommy so flustered that she stopped the paddling and muttered to herself all afternoon.

"What kind of monster child is she, laughing when she's getting punished? Lord Almighty, see what I have to face? Jesus, Mary, Joseph, how can I deal with such children, no feelings, not an ounce of feeling there at all."

Daddy belted Mary Ruth that night for laughing during her punishment. He says it was very disrespectful and that we are supposed to honor our father and mother. It's one of the Ten Commandments, which have something to do with being Catholic. Getting belted by Daddy means, you pull down your pants, and undies, so they're in a little puddle around your ankles. Then you lean over the side of your bed as he undoes his belt buckle and slowly pulls the belt out of the loops. He folds it in two, grasps it in one hand, and taps his empty palm with it. He breathes real hard in and out, in and out as he does this. And so do you. Then he cracks the belt in the air and says, "This hurts me more than it hurts you."

The belt comes down hard on your behind, and you try not to cry too loud because then Daddy will think you don't believe that it hurts him more than it hurts you, and he'll have to hit you harder and harder until you stop making noise. If you're lucky he's done in six whacks. He leaves the room, and you're left to pull up your pants, sniffling and alone.

I don't remember if Kathy got belted for losing the dollar bill. But ever since that day Mommy hasn't sent any of us to the little store. And she always brings the lost dollar bill up, especially when company's over and we're all at the dining room table. I can't tell you how many times I've heard her tell that story, all the while Kathy, Mary Ruth and I are cringing, hoping, praying we can be excused before we have to hear any more.

That's not the only episode that keeps surfacing like poop that won't flush down the toilet. One time we cut Gramma's parlor drapes right up. Now the way Mommy says it, you'd think we meant to wreck Gramma's entire house and the drapes were just the beginning, but that's not how it was at all. We were playing in the parlor and I found a pair of scissors on the table. I started to fiddle with them, and I figured out how to cut some of the threads that were just sticking up loose from the chair I was sitting on.

Kathy and Mary Ruth saw that, and, oh, for a second or so I was queen bee, smile covering half of my face, and the two of them looking like I'd maybe just unlocked the lid to a big box of treasure. But then they swooped down on me like hawks after a rabbit, grabbed the scissors and cut the rest of the loose threads on the arm of the chair. Then they moved to the drapes and started cutting them. It was a beautiful sight just watching this thick burgundy velvet fall gently to the floor. I don't know if I've ever seen anything so graceful before or since. None of us knew the drapes were like Humpty Dumpty and could never be put back together again.

When Gramma found us she was mad at first, but by the time Daddy got home and she showed him the drapes, she wasn't even worked up over it anymore. Daddy got her some new drapes, and she's happy. Really. She hasn't said boo about it since the day it happened. But Mommy, who wasn't even there at the time, can't forget it.

There's another thing she likes to bring up as evidence of my stupidity. She wasn't there then either, but that doesn't stop her. It was the only time in my life I've known Daddy to have a meeting with a priest at a rectory. Kathy, Mary Ruth and I sat on a long, dark wooden bench in a narrow waiting area while he and the priest went into an office nearby and closed the door. We were out there waiting for quite a long time—long enough for me to get really itchy, and squirmy, and bored. Then some nuns, two of them, sat down across from us, their black robes billowing all over their bench. They were as nice and smiling as they could be with their faces all crunched up in those habits. One of them said, "My what lovely little girls waiting so quietly. Why are you here?"

Kathy answered, "Our daddy's talking to the priest." As usual, Mary Ruth and I relied on her to take charge of the situation.

They looked at the closed office door. "Oh, I see," said the talkative nun." She continued her questions.

"Have you been waiting long?"

"Not too long," Kathy replied.

"Well then little ladies, what are your names?"

Kathy said, "Katherine Beatrice." This was long before she hated the name Beatrice. She'd never say it out loud now, and Mary Ruth and I are sworn to keep it secret under penalty of being sat upon and tickled mercilessly, beaten up, bitten, and then ignored for the rest of our lives.

Mary Ruth said, "Mary Ruth."

I was panicking because I'd just recently learned my middle name. I remembered Laura, of course, because that's what everybody's always called me, but I couldn't remember what came next. I just knew it was a long word, so I blurted out "Laura Grasshopper." It was the longest word I could think of, and I hoped it would do.

Kathy and Mary Ruth both whipped their heads around really fast and sneered in perfect unison, "Grasshopper? Your name's not Grasshopper."

The nun who had been quiet until that moment started tittering and giggling. Then she began laughing deep belly laughs right out loud. I was thinking that Kathy and Mary Ruth were right, Grasshopper just didn't sound right after I said it. The talkative nun was trying not to laugh, but she wasn't succeeding. She asked Mary Ruth between giggles, "Then what is her middle name?"

Mary Ruth said, "I don't know. I just know it's not Grasshopper."

Of course, the nuns, with the enthusiastic help of Mary Ruth and Kathy, just had to tell Daddy all about it when he finished with his meeting, and Daddy told Mommy, and now she always brings it up. Always. It's on this long list of things in her head that we've all done wrong, and each time one of us makes a mistake the whole list gets hauled out and rattled off. With it getting longer all the time, I don't know how she can possibly remember it all, but she does. The thing Kathy, Mary Ruth and I try to do is just not make any mistakes—ever.

Sometimes Mommy takes pictures of our punishments. One afternoon she accused me of lying because I said I could remember being in my crib. "Now, Laura, don't lie. Nobody can remember when they were that small," she said.

"But I do. I do. I…"

"I told you to stop lying."

"But I do remember. I remember being in my crib."

"Oh, you do, do you? Well, I'll give you something else to remember. The idea. She thinks she remembers being in her crib. Ha."

She grabbed hold of my arm and yanked me right up next to her. Then she swatted me hard on the behind. At this I started to wail, and she said, "Oh, stop your belly achin'. I didn't hurt you that much." That made me cry even louder.

"I'll give you something to cry about," she snapped. Then she reached down, holding my arm with one hand, and with the other yanking my shorts off and ripping off my blouse. She dragged me through the kitchen and shoved me out the back door. I was screaming my head off by this time. And she said, "I'll teach you to lie, little girl. Get in your sandbox."

She came to the edge of the sandbox and pulled the only bit of clothing I had left on, my undies, down to my ankles. "Stay right there," she ordered as she backed away into the house.

She came back out carrying a camera. Sobbing and screaming, I pulled up my undies, while she snapped pictures of me. Just then our neighbor, Mr. Brown, leaned over the side of the fence that divides our yards and said, "What's the matter, Laura?"

I just kept on sobbing. Mommy put the camera in the pocket of her apron and said in a cheerful voice, "Oh, Mr.

Brown. I just don't know what got into her going outside practically naked. When I told her to pull her pants up, she just started to scream."

One of those pictures is now in our family album along with others from times I was just as upset. When she shows those pictures to visitors—something she loves to do—she talks about me as though I just started crying for no reason. She laughs, and the people she's showing them to laugh. Then Mommy leans close to them and whispers, "These girls can be so difficult at times," and they laugh some more.

I've never seen Grampa Adams smile. Not once. And he's never said one kind thing to me, Kathy or Mary Ruth. I try not to feel bad about that though because he's not nice to Daddy either, or even Mommy. I'm still trying to figure out how Mommy came to belong to him. It seems to me that she should belong to the O'Neills. I don't know why Grampa O'Neill's not Mommy's daddy, unless she has two daddies, which may be possible. I found out that Grampa O'Neill is still mine because of a bad thing that turned out to be a good thing.

One day I was in the bathroom and supposed to be brushing my teeth, and Rusty bit me really hard on the thumb. I had just seen an episode of *Lassie* where some man stole Lassie from Timmy and tied a bandana around her muzzle to keep her quiet. Well, Rusty was right there by that swan-neck-like pipe below the sink. I put my toothbrush down, and I leaned down and wondered if I could do the same thing with Rusty. Since I didn't have a bandana, I thought putting my fingers around his muzzle might work. I lowered my right hand very slowly toward the dog, my thumb and index finger

50

curving to make a C shape. Rusty watched carefully with his brown eyes open wide as I got closer and closer. Then when I got about an inch or so away, snap! There I was crying like crazy with blood streaming out of my thumb in two places.

I came out of the bathroom screaming, and first Mommy started screaming too. She does that whenever one of us gets hurt and runs to her for help. Nowadays I try not to go to her. Back then I wasn't expecting to get yelled at, so I ran straight to her, and she yelled, "Ka—, a Ma— a, Laura, what have you done? What have you done to yourself? I send you in to brush your teeth, and you can't even do that right? Well I'll be, the girl can't even brush her teeth when she's told. What on earth is the matter with you? Are you totally empty upstairs?"

I stood there fidgeting, blood dripping down from my thumb. Eventually she calmed down, and I was able to blurt out between sobs that Rusty bit me. The wonderful upshot of the whole thing was that later that afternoon, the doorbell rang, and in walked Grampa O'Neill with Uncle Dean, and Mommy said I was going to stay with Grampa for a few days, and he was going to take care of my thumb. This was fine by me.

At his house, a couple of times each day, Grampa had me soak my hand in a bowl of hot water with some medicine stuff he poured in. There was always a dime in there too. Grampa said if I kept my hand in until he told me I could take it out, I got to keep the dime. So, of course, I kept it in because I love dimes. They're my absolutely favorite kind of money.

When I wasn't soaking my hand, I was visiting with all of the O'Neills who live with Grampa. Aunt Ruth and Uncle Dean were there, and they were really nice to me. Aunt Ruth let me play with some beautiful bracelets, pins and necklaces in a box in her room, and Uncle Dean took me to the park. He ran with me around the playground and laughed so much I fell into his arms laughing too, not like when we went to visit Mantino. Sometimes Aunt Bea and Uncle Jim stopped in too. They used to live at Grampa's, but then they each got married and started their own homes.

Gramma O'Neill was there too. She was still in bed with her bad heart, and I had to walk into the room once quietly and say hi to her. Uncle Rol, Gramma O'Neill's brother, lives in the big house now too. When I couldn't get to sleep at night because of all the traffic whizzing by on Garfield Boulevard, he came in and sprinkled holy water on the sheets of the bed I was trying to sleep in. It didn't really help me get to sleep, but I like that he did it anyway.

Uncle Rol and I walked to a church one day to visit God. The stairs were lighter than the sand at Lake Michigan. And they were so wide I couldn't step right from one to another. I had to take an extra step across each stair. The inside was so beautiful with stained glass windows all full of different colors with the sun shining through them. We went to the side of the sanctuary where the candles in deep red holders are all lined up in neat little rows. Uncle Rol lit some of them. As he lit the last one he said, "This one is for your mother, Laura. Say a little prayer with me."

So I knelt down and bent my head and tried to think really kind thoughts about Mommy. Uncle Rol seemed really sad, and it made me feel sad too. Even so, I wanted to stay inside next to Uncle Rol and just look at the candles flickering in the dim light. But after a little while Uncle Rol said we had to get back to Grampa's. Then pretty soon I had to go home.

Mommy's not always mean. She's happy when Daddy's home, when we have company over, and when we go out visiting too. These are some really good times. It's just when she's got us at home to deal with on her own that I guess we get out of hand, and we drive her to do her cat thing.

One of the times we have the most fun is when we're riding in Kaisery. I love Kaisery, love that this beautiful pink car is part of our family. I love riding in the back seat with Kathy and Mary Ruth. We've been on the road for ages now because it's a long way to Hinsdale. We're each settled into our separate thoughts, done with our fighting for the time being, watching everything go by so fast outside the window

The first time I ever sang was in the back seat of Kaisery, right behind Daddy, where I am now. I just jumped in on the chorus to *Jimmy Crack Corn*. That's usually one of the first songs we do. Daddy sings the verses and then Kathy, Mary Ruth and I sing the chorus at the top of our lungs, and nobody minds, not even Mommy when she's riding up in the front seat next to Daddy. We sing *Somewhere Over the Rainbow, Little Brown Jug, I've Got Six Pence, Big Rock Candy Mountain*, and so many others. Often at night, when Kathy, Mary Ruth and I are so tired we can't sing another note, Daddy will end it all with *Three Coins in a Fountain*. It almost makes me cry when he sings it, this strong feeling just fills me up, and then sometimes I fall asleep right there in Kaisery.

Mommy doesn't sing along in the car because she says our kind of singing isn't really music. But she doesn't cover her ears either because when Daddy's happy, it's hard for everybody around him not to catch it. That's something I adore about him.

Mommy's something called a classical musician. So is Grampa Adams. She plays piano and he plays bass. And he used to play cello with some symphony somewhere, but he doesn't anymore. He's retired. But he still has his bass and it's almost as tall as he is and three times as wide. I hope that someday I can be as good on the piano as Mommy is. Her playing is like magic too, come to think of it. She has this whole repertoire of things. Some of them are happy marches, and Mary Ruth and I can't help dancing all around the living room when she plays them. Kathy has two trick knees, so she doesn't always join in. She watches, head tilted to the side, and Mommy says she's like Lady Godiva. And it seems Mommy has a piano piece for every sort of mood and every sort of character. Like there's this music from this thing called *Peter and the Wolf*, and when she plays one part she'll ask, "Can't you just see Peter skipping along to this?" and I can, I really can. And then she plays a very different sort of music sort of scary, and she asks, "Now can't you see the wolf coming?" and I really can see the wolf coming too.

I love all of the pieces she plays, the concertos, the mazurkas, the sonatas, the fugues. All of them are wonderful, but I think I like *Rustle of Spring* the best. People always ask her to play it when they visit. I feel lucky to be there when that happens. We snuggle in on the couch, and it's like we all enter a dream. The piece builds and builds like when I stack wooden blocks one on top of the other higher and higher. Except her playing is better than that. I get more and more swept away like spring is stirring in my own body each time and, oh, I'm in love with the world. And when she finishes and the last notes are still there in the air, everyone in the room is silent. We stay silent for a long time because the same thing has happened to each of us and we can't think of the right words to say.

Finally, one of the adults will say something like, "That was magnificent, Helen." And then the room will slowly fill with conversation, like the way a summer shower starts slow at first with just a few drops and then grows stronger until rain is falling lightly everywhere, beading on the flowers and leaves, running down my face and into my wide-open mouth. And then a rainbow forms across the sky, and what could be more beautiful? At those times I think I must have the most amazing mommy in all of Chicago.

I can't wait until I can do that myself—play piano in a way that gets a whole room full of people breathless and amazed. Right now I'm working on getting the C scale so I play it in a nice even tempo up and down, up and down, up and down, without jerking or stopping or hitting any wrong notes. I'm also learning a beautiful song, *To a Wild Rose*, but Mommy says it'll be a while before I'm ready to play that for company.

I've gotten used to hearing grown-ups call Mommy Helen. The first time I noticed that Mommy has this other name was when my godmother, Aunt Irene, came to visit and say goodbye because she was moving all the way out of Illinois somewhere. During the visit, Aunt Irene called Mommy Helen. I wondered why. After Aunt Irene left I asked, "How come Aunt Irene calls you Helen and I call you Mommy?"

Mommy just about had a conniption fit saying, "What, Mommy isn't good enough for you? You want to call me Helen now? I guess you think you don't need a mother, if you want to go call me Helen. Well go ahead call me Helen, see if I care."

I tried to say to her that I didn't want to call her Helen. It was just the first time I realized she had a name other than Mommy. It didn't mean I wanted to call her something else. She wouldn't let me get a word in.

Pretty soon after that I found out that Daddy has another name too; it's Henry, but most people call him Hank. And Gramma's name is Mary, but people used to call her Mamie when she was young. Grampa O'Neill's name is Eugene, just like Uncle Dean's whose really named Eugene after Grampa, but everybody calls him Dean instead of Eugene. And it was around that time when I figured out we have last names too.

I thought my last name was O'Neill, and that's what I told Mommy.

She said, "For cryin' out loud, Laura O'Neill? Where did you get that stupid idea? Your name is Laura Gross, Laura Elizabeth Gross.

"Gross?"

"Yes, Gross.

The name just sort of went thud, thud, thump inside of me, like a rock. I told Mommy, "That's not a pretty name like O'Neill, and how come my name isn't O'Neill?"

She replied, "Gross is your father's name and Gramma's name, and if it's good enough for them it's certainly good enough for the likes of you."

"I don't like it. Can I have a different name?"

"It's a good German name Laura. Your father's half German and half Irish. It means big or important because your ancestors were some big deal landowners once upon a time. The name used to be von Gross back in Germany, but the family shortened it here, didn't want to put on airs.

Gross also means twelve dozen; that's the number 144. You'll understand more about that when you learn arithmetic in school, if you're not too slow to learn, that is."

"How did Gramma and Daddy get the name Gross?" I asked.

Mommy said, "Your grandmother married your grandfather and took his last name. That's what women do when they get married."

"What did her name used to be?"

"It was McHale, Laura. Gramma used to be Mary Frances McHale, and now she's Mary Frances Gross."

I thought to myself that she should have kept McHale. "Oh," I said, "Is your name Gross too?"

"Yes, and it used to be Adams."

"How come it didn't used to be O'Neill?" I asked.

"That's enough of your questions now, Laura. I have other things to do."

"But—"

"Oh, stop with the buts. Go on outside and try to rake some leaves why don't you. For Christ's sake. I never heard of such a thing, a child not liking her own family name. You'd better get moving quick before I tell your father. You know the rules."

Rules. Now that I'm five years old and almost all the way through kindergarten, I really do get what rules are, and I'm learning how not to break them. It's taken a lot of spankings and beltings for me to get to this place of knowing. I figured out that in our house there's just one main rule. That is, do what you're told. It's like the potato when I play Mr. Potato Head. It's the main thing, the thing that the other rules, the eyes, nose, mouth and ears get stuck to. Now the parts that really complete the potato are, drop what you're doing this instant and do what you're told, not when you happen to get around to it. And another piece is, don't express any feelings about what you're told to do unless they're cheerful ones. And then another piece is, do a perfect job even if you've never done it before.

Following the rules is the most important thing. That's why this very morning when Daddy opened up Kaisery's back door, held his arm out toward me and then swooped it toward the car and told me to get in, I jumped right up from the grass where I was looking for a four-leaf clover and climbed right inside. He's so happy today that he practically danced to the car. That's another thing I love about Daddy, the way he just up and starts dancing and leaping up and clicking his heels together when he's happy. Kathy and Mary Ruth got in the car right after I did, and he got in and said we were going off to Hinsdale.

I wonder what the house looks like now that it's almost finished. I can't imagine ever being able to build a house; they're so big and complicated. You should hear Mommy and Gramma talk about this on Sundays. They are impressed! You can see the pride practically splitting apart the seams of their dresses when they talk about it.

"You know there isn't anything my Hank can't do when he sets his mind to it," says Gramma.

"Oh, and to think, he and John just saw the plans in a magazine one day and said, 'Let's do it,' as if it's as easy as taking out the trash, you know," Mommy adds.

"My, my, my, a new home. And in a community as nice as Hinsdale."

"Great public school too for the girls, much better than Darwin, Hank says."

"Fine Catholic school there too, I hear."

"Most likely, but Hank wants them in public school."

"It's a shame, that is."

I'm proud of Daddy and Unc too for doing such an amazing thing, but I don't really see what's wrong with our house on Richmond Street, or our block, or our school, Darwin Elementary. I love it there, even though I wanted to go to the Catholic school with Charlie at first, since I'm Catholic and all. But once I set foot inside the classroom, I felt completely at ease. It's big and full of this soft, warm light, like the sunlight in Grampa O'Neill's upstairs that comes through the curtains and dances just so on the carpets in the late afternoon. It's a kind of sunlight that lets you stand still and breathe nice and deep for a second or two. And the room is full of kids from all over the world. Just standing in line waiting to collect our milk one day, a girl from Germany told me the German words for star and morning. And another time in line a boy taught me the Spanish words for milk and cookies. I don't remember the words now, but hearing them and knowing there are all these different ways to say the same thing was like dancing in a rainbow.

Sometimes in school we have circle time and we make things. Like one day we made butter. We passed around a mayonnaise jar full of cream. Each one of us had to shake it a little bit and pass it on. After a few times around the circle, it was butter, and we each had some on Saltines. We've got a log cabin in our room too. That's lots of fun to play in. And the best thing about my class is that we're practicing to be a band for our big graduation show. Some of us are playing tambourines, sticks, bells. I'm in the triangle group, and we all play our instruments when the teacher tells us to. It sounds really nice.

Mary Ruth graduated last year, and Kathy did the year before. I was up in the balcony with Mommy both times watching them. Each of them wore a real cap and gown and walked across the stage to get a diploma from the school's principal. Their graduation pictures and diplomas are in the family album now.

This year it'll be my turn, and maybe everybody will be watching me. But then I'll have to say good-bye to my classmates for good because we're moving to Hinsdale. I'll miss the whole class because everybody in class is everybody else's friend. It's like no matter how we are grouped together, we're all happy because everybody's fun to be with, except sometimes there's these two boys who fight about who's going to sit with me. If I sit next to one, the other sticks out his tongue at me, and the same thing happens if I sit with the other. I'm just glad it doesn't happen every day. I like them both as much as the other kids in class, but not as much as I like Charlie.

I hear a racket below. It's Kaisery's tires going over little bitty stones called gravel. We just turned a corner. I recognize this crunch, crunchy street. It's not smooth like Richmond Street. I hope we'll have potatoes baked in a fire outside like we did the last time we visited here. I don't know if I've ever eaten anything as good as fire-baked potatoes with lots of butter and salt.

Daddy's pulling into our driveway now. It's gravel too. Right next to us is a great big truck with great big men, wider and taller by far than Daddy. They are carrying things out of the truck, across the dirt yard, and over a plank leading to our front door. I can hear Mommy's voice inside. We left Richmond Street before she did, but she and Grampa Adams got here first because we stopped at some building supply place to buy parts to our new doorbell.

One of the things they're carrying is the dining room table that Grampa Adams built. I recognize it because it has a little bit of green tint to the varnish, and it's got lots of cool curves around the edge of the top and on the legs too. I can't image being able to make a table any more than making a house. I wonder what we're going to eat on when we get back to Richmond Street. I guess we could use the kitchen table. It's almost as big as the dining room table.

Daddy says, "Go inside girls, and take a look around."

So I head to the plank. He says we'll have front stairs and a porch soon, but for now it's just a plank over a pit. The plank is really wobbly, and it's muddy below. Kathy and Mary Ruth dart across. I hold my breath, close my eyes, and follow at full speed. Inside, Daddy's so excited he seems to be spinning around in all sorts of directions at once. He tells us what room is what, talking fast like a man I saw on Kedzie Avenue who was fishing for people on the sidewalk, trying to talk them into going inside of his appliance store. The dining room table's in the dining room, of course, just off the kitchen. The kitchen has lots of light wood colored cabinets. They're almost yellow. Mommy's in there unloading dishes, our dishes. I recognize the so-thick-they're-almost-unbreakable light yellow, green and blue plastic bowls and plates. Mommy points to something on a countertop. "Look at the stove, girls," she says, "the burners pull out from the wall."

She says this like she's just won a trip to Niagara Falls, where she and Daddy went on their honeymoon. She tells us we can take turns pulling them down and up again if we're careful. When I get my turn, I think they're pretty cool. It's fun to have something like a stovetop just disappear into a wall. It's just like my daddy to think of something like that.

Then I hear his voice calling, "Come on girls. Your room's at the end of the hall." I rush out of the kitchen, down the hall to the room at the end. I see Kathy and Mary Ruth's bunk beds have been split up so they're two regular beds side by side. Right next to them, third in the row is my little bed, with the lumpy plastic covered mattress. It is so uncomfortable, you wouldn't believe it. But Mommy says there's no way I'm going to get a regular mattress until I stop peeing in my bed at night.

This is an awful thing that I do. I don't mean to do it. It just happens, not all the time, but every couple of months. Mommy and Daddy have no patience for this, especially since Kathy and Mary Ruth never had this problem. I try not to do it, but usually I'll be sound asleep, and in my dream I have to pee really bad. I'm looking everywhere, everywhere for a toilet, and I can't find one. I find bathrooms that have sinks, and sometimes they even have toilet paper, but no toilets. Then after a long time of searching, finally I find a bathroom with a toilet. I pull my pants down, sit on the toilet seat, relax, and I start to pee.

Then I wake up, and I'm peeing in bed, and it's too late to stop. The warm liquid is spreading out beneath me, and it feels like all of my happiness is spreading out of me too because all I can do is lie there knowing Mommy will notice first thing in the morning because she always checks. She'll call Daddy, and he'll get out his belt. There's no getting around that. And I have to think about this all the rest of the night as the mattress, the sheet, and my pajamas grow colder with each passing minute.

I stare at my bed in the new bedroom. I wonder what we're going to sleep on back at Richmond Street if our beds are here. I wonder why there's green and gray tile on the floor. It's really icky. I wonder where the upstairs to our new house is too. Richmond Street has an upstairs. You get to it using a narrow little stairway near the front door. It's just one little room where tiny rays of light squeak through the half-closed shutters on the room's only window. Mommy sews up there, and sometimes she lets me watch her, but she says I can't touch any of the paper bags up there because there are baby alligators inside. I don't touch a thing. I wouldn't want to let a bunch of alligators loose in the house. Even though I hardly ever go upstairs, I like having an upstairs. A house doesn't seem like a house unless it has one.

Just as I'm wondering about all this, Daddy joins us in the room and Kathy says, "Daddy, is there another floor somewhere?"

"No, this is a ranch house. It's just what your mother wanted. She doesn't want to go running up and down stairs keeping track of you girls."

So there you have it. Mommy wants a ranch house, and

that's what we get, like it or not. I know I should be happy about this. I mean Daddy built this house, and I am proud of that. The wood outside is redwood, and it's really pretty. Mommy says "redwood" like she's just been given a mink stole or something. And I can see why. It is nice, really it is. And I don't know how many other fathers could just see the plans for a house in a magazine one day and pretty soon just up and build one. But still I'm a little bit disappointed with this ranch house thing. I feel like I'm very bad for feeling that way.

I hear a high-pitched, almost sad sort of sound far off. I like it a lot. It's mysterious. Daddy says it's a train whistle for the Burlington Northern line. He says the tracks are about seven long blocks away, and the trains go to and from Chicago. Imagine that, living near enough to train tracks to walk to them. Mommy comes into the room and asks, "Do you think the girls will have a hard time sleeping tonight with the train whistle going like that?"

And Daddy says, "No, it's too far away. They'll barely hear it. Besides they'll sleep like logs, most likely, tired from all the excitement of the move."

I look down at my scuffed brown shoes that are practically worn out from running up and down the Richmond Street sidewalk.

Then Mommy says, "And girls, here's some really good news for you. You're on summer vacation now. No more school until September. The schools get out a week earlier here than in the city."

I feel heat burn my cheeks. I'm sure my face is turning beet red. I rush outside to think about all of this. Standing there in the dirt that will soon be our front lawn, I realize that

I'm here to stay. I'm not going back to live on Richmond Street ever again, and I'm never going to have my kindergarten graduation, never going to play the triangle in our band. It must not be important, if it's not worth staying in the city for. No cap and gown for me, no good-byes to my friends at school, no good-bye to Charlie, no last little walks to see old Mrs. Piccolo in her rocking chair. No more going to the little store to walk down the stairs past those old men and their cigars to look at candy. No more Charlie in the yard each morning asking, "Can Laura come out and play?"

I feel as bleak as the dirt under my feet. Daddy calls out "Come to the backyard girls. There's a beautiful sunset." I get up and walk around the side of the house to the big empty space that will be our backyard. And I look up into the sky. I can see that it is gorgeous—all different shades of pink, purple, orange, blue and gray—all across the sky. I don't think I've ever really noticed a sunset before, not like this. I wish Charlie were here with us. It's almost as wonderful as the water lilies on the lake. Then Mommy calls from the kitchen, "Time for supper, girls. Go wash up and help set the table."

Kathy, Mary Ruth and I crowd together in the bathroom to wash our hands. It's narrow, and we keep bumping into each other. The cabinets are the same almost yellow wood as in the kitchen. I open one up, and it's already full of Band-Aids, washcloths, toilet paper, towels.

I help set the table, carrying our dinner plates and platters of cold cuts from the kitchen to the dining room—silverware, napkins, glasses of milk too. When everything's ready, we sit down. Daddy says the regular bless-us-oh-Lord prayer, and then says "and bless our new home too," before he ends with "Amen." Then we start passing things around. I'm spreading some mustard on my bread—and Daddy says you always have to spread your condiments on the bread, not on the lunch meat—when Mommy says, "You know, Laura's a very mean girl."

That gets everybody's attention. Knives in the air, hands frozen reaching for bread or on a dish of coleslaw. She's called me stupid, slow, and retarded so much, hardly anyone notices when she says that. But mean? She's never said that before. We all look at her. She's smiling her cat smile again as she continues, "Yes, she's mean all right. Charlie came to say good-bye to her. There he was at the door, and I had to tell him that Laura was already gone. Imagine that. She didn't even bother to say good-bye to her best friend. He was heartbroken."

We all just sit quietly taking it in. I just keep looking at my knife, and Mommy says, "What do you have to say for yourself, Laura?"

I'm thinking I should have known we were moving today. All the signs were there. I realize that now. Mommy and Daddy were talking together about how to pack everything and asking each other how was our parakeet, Twinker, going to travel and everything. But all I knew was it was coming soon. Now if I tell everyone I didn't know today was the day, if I tell them I thought we were moving after my kindergarten graduation, they'll all laugh at me.

"Well Laura," Mommy bores in on me. I just can't look at her. I just can't look up at anybody. I want this whole day to go away, "Cat got your tongue, Laura?" she goads. I can't look up.

Finally Grampa Adams, grouchy, mean old Grampa Adams, says, "Ahh leave girl alone ehh, Helen."

And then Daddy says, "Yeah, I guess Charlie's just the first of many hearts she'll break."

And then Mommy, still smiling says, "Well, I guess that means we don't have to worry about taking you to visit him. That's a relief to me. It's such a long way."

"Yeah," Daddy says, "It'd be nuts to want to go back to that run-down neighborhood anyway. All we could want is here. There will be plenty of kids on this block to play with."

And I think plenty of kids, sure, but not like Charlie. I wish I could tell him I'm sorry for not saying good-bye, tell him that I didn't know we were moving today. But there's no way I can reach him now, and Charlie's going to have to live forever thinking I'm just a cruel girl who thought so little of all the good times we had that I couldn't bother to look him in the eye and say good-bye before I got into Kaisery and rode out of his life. Better that though than my family having more proof of how stupid I really am.

I was an especially good Catholic girl. I wrote essays for the school papers, presided over club meetings with a gavel, listened gracefully, dressed tastefully, and kept everything neat and clean, always, a good Catholic girl. I was the one closest to Jesus, everybody always said so. It's just that when it was all coming to a close, when I was supposed to dedicate my being, my self, everything I was to God, I thought just for a while to postpone my fate. What harm could it do to go to teachers college instead of joining the sisters, first at Mundelein, then St. Mary-of-the-Woods? My father and mother asked me to reconsider. My future had been planned for years. Surely I'd be happier studying with the sisters at Mundelein, wouldn't I? But in the end they relented. I lived at home and brought my faith with me to public college.

Mary Agnes

Adjustments

If anyone asked me what I thought, and if I was sure that nobody would burst into spit-filled giggles or belt me for my answer, I would say that as far as I'm concerned Hinsdale, Illinois, is for the birds. But Mommy and Daddy love it here, that's for sure. There's an air of excitement all around us when they talk about all the stuff Mommy and Grampa Adams planted last summer and all the final touches Daddy has planned for the house. It's nice to be around all of this happiness.

Daddy's around more now because before we moved he was spending all of his free time here without us. Now we're here with him. He's downstairs a lot in the basement. He set up part of it as a workroom. Sometimes when he's sawing boards over his sawhorse, I hold the end of the board for him to keep it from splitting and breaking off as the jagged blade goes back and forth over the wood. Daddy says my holding the board helps make it a nice, clean cut. I like that, just being down there helping him.

Mommy likes to brag about how big our yard is. She says it's 75 feet across, and most of the lots are 50 feet across. Ours is the second widest lot. The widest one belongs to a big house across the street, two stories, white with black shutters. It's on an entire acre, with three big trees in front, even bigger than the ones on Richmond Street.

Across the street there are lots of trees, big elm and oak trees, and some of the houses are two stories. The others are ranch houses like ours, except older and shaded by the trees. All the homes on our side of the street are new and flat, and there's not one tree, except for little ones we've all been planting. That's because until not too long ago this was farmland. We put in a cherry tree in front and a rose of Sharon bush, salvia and forsythia along our driveway, sweet peas in front of the house by one of the basement windows. Soon we'll plant some sort of hedge, but none of this, even the cherry tree, is going to ever grow tall and provide much shade like the trees across the street. So there won't be that wonderful arch of trees over the road like on Richmond Street.

Out back Mommy and Grampa Adams planted an apple tree in the side yard near the clothesline, and right behind the house Daddy planted a linden tree and an ash tree. There are going to be more trees and a garden in back too where the alley is supposed to be. That's a strange thing about this place. There are no alleys, so one yard just melts into another in the back unless people plant hedges to separate themselves, which Mommy says we're going to do at some point. It'll be a thorny rose bush hedge all across the back of our yard.

We put out bags and bags of grass seed, all around the house. Some of it sprouted into real nice grass, but it's so thin, sort of like the hair on Grampa Adams' head. He's not bald, like Grampa O'Neill, but you can see the skin of his scalp through his hair in lots of places. That's how our lawn is. But Mommy says this year it'll be a lot thicker and that I just need to be patient. Most of our neighbors put in sod. It comes all rolled up like ice cream cake, and it's in wide strips. All you have to do is roll it out, and you have an instant lawn. And it's nice and thick and even. Mommy says it's way too expensive for the likes of us. She did splurge on the grass seed for one side of the house. It's Kentucky blue grass. When we threw the seeds on the dirt she said it was going to be a deep blue-green, much prettier than any other grass around, including the sod that our neighbors have. But when it grew in, it looked pretty much the same as the other grass to me. But since Mommy says it's special, when I go out, I pretend it's blue-green. When I do that I feel like I'm in a very special place.

When Mommy talks about the blue grass she also says that when she was smaller than me she lived for a short time in Kentucky. It's a state below Illinois and a little bit to the right on a map. She smiles really wide and sweet and talks just for a little bit, like when you take a little taste of soup to see if it needs more salt or something before you serve it.

"I was really happy. We lived on a farm, and I remember picking strawberries and eating them right there on the spot. Umm, they were good."

"What else did you do?" I ask.

"Oh, I don't really remember. We didn't stay there long."

"Why?"

"We had to move to Wisconsin."

"But why?"

"That's none of your beeswax."

71

Laura McHale Holland

Wisconsin is the state right above Illinois on the map. Mommy's not as happy when she says Wisconsin as when she says Kentucky. It's like Kentucky is a chocolate sundae placed right in front of you on a warm summer day, and Wisconsin is a container of cottage cheese that's been sitting in the back of the refrigerator too long growing mold. I wish she could have stayed longer in Kentucky where she was happy.

Having all this space around the house seems odd to me, although I am getting used to it. Even the houses on lots that are narrower than ours have wide spaces between them. I step outside, and with all this space and no trees, I feel like a fly crawling on a window pane, really wide open for anyone to swat me. On Richmond Street, the space between houses was only wide enough for a path to walk down from front to back. I guess the alley and sidewalks chopped things up too. Same with Gramma's. Even though the buildings are enormous, there's just a little space between each of them. I like those little spaces. I feel like the buildings are hugging me.

We don't have sidewalks here either, and the street and our driveway aren't hard and smooth. They're made from gravel. You can always tell when a car rolls down the street. The wheels crunching the gravel sound louder than the engine of the car to me.

It's a funny thing about all this space though. When Daddy and Grampa Adams put a couple of stakes by the side of our property to mark where one of our hedges is going to end, Mr. Reid came out and told Daddy our stakes were sticking over the property line. They had a big discussion about it, and neither one of them was happy. I thought, what does it matter, with all this space? What's a foot here or there one way or another? Daddy and Mr. Reid each consulted their official papers where the property lines are drawn. I'm sure Daddy was right. He always is. It was the man who had built the house for Mr. Reid who must have made a mistake. I feel bad for Mr. Reid that he doesn't know how to build his own house like Daddy does. Ever since then, I guess you'd say we've been on cooler terms with the Reids. Mommy's made friends with Mrs. Dearden, the mom of the family on the other side of our property, even calls her by her first name, Mildred. But if she knows Mrs. Reid's first name, she's not saying it.

The Reids have a bunch of kids, and the oldest is a boy named Dale. He's in kindergarten. He used to come over to our yard to see if I'd play with him, but I didn't want to play with anyone except Charlie. Dale's too little anyway to be my special, special friend. Even though I didn't graduate from kindergarten, officially, I started first grade last fall, so I'm a whole year ahead of him. Sometimes we play together when all the kids on the block are getting together for a game of bounce or fly or hide-and-seek.

The Deardens have two children, a boy named Walter who's a year older than Kathy—that makes him ancient to me—and they have a girl named Bonnie who's Mary Ruth's age. Bonnie had us over for a tea party just before school started. We sat outside on their driveway at a card table, one of us in a chair at each side. Mrs. Dearden brought out 7 Up for us in teacups and little ham sandwiches made with bread cut in quarters with the crust cut off. Mommy says taking the crust off is very wasteful. But those sandwiches sure were cute, and just the right size for our hands. Then we had peanut butter cookies. Mrs. Dearden took pictures of us too, and now we've got a picture of us at our tea party in the family album. That's a lot better than the punishment pictures Mommy put in from Richmond Street.

Another good thing about being here is that Unc comes over on weekends and helps Daddy finish things off. They used concrete for our front stairs and porch, and they used it to make this thick wall between our property and the Dearden's because our house is right at the bottom of a hill that begins about two blocks up. Now, where the street is, the hill comes to a gradual end. But in the back of our property it drops off like a tiny cliff from the Dearden's yard to ours. Daddy said if he didn't put a wall in, their yard would just fall into ours in no time.

Another great thing about having Unc come over is that sometimes on Sundays instead of us driving to Gramma's house, Unc will bring her here for a visit. She thinks this house is wonderful too. There, I must be out of my head to not appreciate it more. I still get to spend some time real close to Gramma at each visit. We like to sit at the dining room table and look out the window to the house across the street. There's an old woman living there. Her name is Laura, like mine, but I've never met her. I thought my name belonged just to me, but I was wrong. Sometimes I see her sitting in her window looking out into her yard, and I hope she's nice, since she has the same name as me. But she doesn't smile, and I think maybe she should meet Grampa Adams. Maybe they'd get along since neither one of them smiles.

I mentioned this idea to Mommy and she said, "Oh, no, Grampa Adams doesn't want to meet anybody. He had one great love in his life and that was my mother. God bless her soul. She had high blood pressure, you know, high as a kite. And she fell down dead right on the kitchen floor. Her face was beet red right before it happened. She was high strung, you see. One minute she was patting down the crust for a rhubarb pie and screamin' to high heaven at the top of her lungs about something or other, and the next, well, then she was gone. My dad's never been the same."

I wonder, if her Mommy dropped dead from screaming, why does Mommy do so much of it herself? I would be afraid that it would kill me too, but maybe it doesn't work like that. When Mommy gets going her words gush out like lava from a volcano, and there's no place to run.

Grampa Adams isn't a screamer, just a grumpy, stumpy old man. I guess he's adjusting to life in Hinsdale, like it or not, just like me. He spends a lot of time out back creating a garden. We had peas and lettuce and carrots. Next we're going to have corn, and beans and sunflowers and maybe even a grape arbor. He says we'll have a whole row of fruit trees too—plum, peach and cherry in front of the garden to separate it from the yard. He also says if Kathy, Mary Ruth and I are good and learn how to weed really well, we can each have our own little patch. In the backyard at Richmond Street there wasn't space to even consider something like that, so I guess that's another thing to like about being here.

We go to Madison School, and it's a short, quiet walk to the schoolyard. That's another thing Mommy is really happy about. She gloats on the phone with her friends, telling them how she doesn't have to worry about what Kathy, Mary Ruth and I are up to on our way to and from school.

I loved our walk to Darwin School in the city, so I'm not

that keen on the school being so close. Kathy, Mary Ruth and I would walk down big, wide streets with storefronts full of new and used washers and dryers, televisions, radios, as well as the giant-sized boxes they were packed in, hats and ties, jewelry and handbags, fancy dresses—all kinds of interesting things. And people would see us walking together and smile. One old woman with twinkling blue eyes used to tell us we looked like three little steps when we lined up in a row in front of her. The best part of the walk for me though was seeing the parachute jump ride from Riverview amusement park sticking way high up into the sky. Every day even in the middle of winter when the park was closed, it was this grand reminder of a world of fast rides and a house of horrors, and games, and ducks to feed in the little lake right in the middle of the excitement. Mommy says we can still go to Riverview once a year in the summer. But it's not the same when you can't see the parachute ride every day.

A good thing about being so near our school is that Mommy lets Kathy, Mary Ruth and me walk there sometimes to play on the playground when school's not in session. There are swings and a jungle gym and a merry-go-round type of thing. It's round and spins, and you can climb on it. You can either push off the ground with your feet while you're going around or you can take hold of one of the handles and run around and build up speed and then jump on. Oooh wee, does that ever put the butterflies in your stomach!

All of the playground equipment at Madison School is on grass that is silky soft, except for where it's worn to dirt in some spots. That's probably nicer than the paved playgrounds at Darwin School. It's fun to get going as high as you can on a swing and then jump off, fly through the air and land on the grass way far out from the swings. We keep pumping harder to get higher than we ever have and then jump farther and farther. Landing in the grass makes this not very risky at all. I'd be more careful if I were jumping onto blacktop or gravel. Gravel would be the worst. So I guess the grass all around is another thing to like about this place.

Madison School is smaller than Darwin. It only goes through fifth grade, and Darwin goes all the way through eighth. Madison is just two floors in the shape of maybe three giant alphabet blocks stuck together. But it's a pretty building made out of red brick with lots of white trim. It's set way back at an angle at the corner where Sixth and Madison streets come together. There's a really wide, long sidewalk leading to the huge double doors in front. There are doors like that at the ends on either side too. Daddy says it's colonial style just like the building downtown that has the library on one end and the village hall on the other. That building is at the top of a hill, and from the library windows you can see the train station right below. A lot of buildings downtown are in this colonial style. Daddy says it's one of the things that sets Hinsdale apart, the rules that so many buildings have to be like famous buildings back east somewhere.

"It gives the community some charm, like some thought went into it," he says, "not like some of these other suburbs that let people slap things together any old way."

I thought he might be talking about a place called Villa Park because that's where Daddy had a lot that Gramma gave him. Daddy and Mommy got rid of it though and bought the lot here in Hinsdale to replace it. I've heard Mommy say on the phone how Villa Park just wasn't the right place. "It didn't have the proper sewer service," she says, "and it was so far from Uncle Jack and Aunt Dorothy in Downers Grove. I told Hank that if we moved out of the city I wanted to be close to them so we could visit."

If Mommy wanted to be near Uncle Jack and Aunt Dorothy Rusa so much, I don't know why we didn't just move right to Downers Grove, but I guess maybe Hinsdale must be a better place for some reason. And we do go visit the Rusas a lot. Mommy's mommy, the screamer, was Uncle Jack's sister, so their children are all Mommy's cousins. But sometimes Mommy says her only real cousins are Muriel, who has a big family on the south side of Chicago, and Lucille who has a small family—just her husband and a boy Danny who's a little older than Kathy. Lucille and her family live way outside of the city in a place surrounded by farms. There's even more open space around there than here. Mommy says Danny is not a good boy, not the kind of boy she'd like any of us to marry. I don't know why, and I don't know what makes Muriel and Lucille real cousins when all the children of Uncle Jack and Aunt Dorothy are not.

Visiting Downers Grove is a heap of fun for Kathy, Mary Ruth and me. First of all because we don't have any chores to do the whole time we're there, and second because Uncle Jack and Aunt Dorothy have more space around their house than anybody I've ever known—27 acres! Mommy goes inside to talk to Aunt Dorothy the whole time we're there, and Kathy, Mary Ruth and I stay outside. When we need to pee we use a creepy little outhouse. It smells sort of like leaves that have been rotting in a puddle for a long time, and it's got daddy-long-leg spiders, big horse flies and other creepy things mucking about. That's what I can see anyway. I never look into the big hole in the board we sit over to use like a toilet because I don't want to know what lives down there.

Once per visit we get called in to have some milk and something that Aunt Dorothy has baked. Usually it's this sweet bread with a crunchy crust that's really good. I like to load it up with as much butter as I can without getting it so thick that someone will call me a glutton.

Grampa Adams drives to Uncle Jack's in his old 1936 Nash. He loves that car. It's gray and sort of plump and round, and way high off the ground compared to Kaisery. In good weather he spends part of each day wiping it down with rags, filling little rust spots in with putty, and just poking around in the engine with the hood up. When he has the engine running, it shakes and gets real hot, and there's a fan in there whirring around to try to cool it down. If we're quiet, he lets Kathy, Mary Ruth and me play on the car's running boards. We pretend that the car's zooming down the highway and we're barely hanging on. Sometimes we get so excited we actually do fall off and scrape ourselves on the gravel, but since it's not a long fall, it's nothing to sniffle about.

Sometimes, when Grampa Adams isn't looking, I poke my fingers in the putty. I know I'm not supposed to do this because it leaves little dents, and Grampa Adams wants a nice smooth surface, but it just feels so good to poke that putty in I can't resist. He always goes over the putty a few times anyway, and when I'm sure he's done for the day, I leave it alone so it can dry and get hard. Then in a day or two he paints it the same dark gray color as the rest of the car.

Back on Richmond Street the old Nash was kept in the garage, and Grampa Adams had to drive it through the alley to get it in there. Kaisery was at the curb in front of the house. Here Kaisery is kept in the garage, and Grampa's Nash is outside next to the garage. Daddy says he'll get around to making Grampa something called a carport. He drew me a picture of one on a napkin, and it looks like a garage minus just about everything except the roof. But Daddy has a whole list of things he has to do, including make Mommy a powder room, which is a bathroom minus the bathtub where she can powder her nose in peace. I've never actually seen Mommy powder her nose, but then Kathy, Mary Ruth, and I aren't allowed to go into Mommy and Daddy's bedroom—ever. She may do her powdering in there.

Uncle Jack cleared the land right around his house for yards and meadows, vegetable gardens and a little orchard, leaving just a few beautiful trees for shade. Then a whole lot of the land is cleared part way, so maybe there are half as many trees as in the dense woods nearby, maybe even less, but there's still lots of trees. There are a couple of deep ravines too running through the property, and we pretend there's water in them, and we're sailing away on great big ships. We just go from one adventure to another.

Sometimes there are baby frogs jumping all across the meadow. There are so many you don't have to be fast to catch one. All you have to do is bend down in the tall grass, cup your hand, take aim just when you see one land, and put it down right over the frog. They are so cute. Kathy, Mary Ruth and I love every one of them. We grab hold just enough to get them on our palms and watch the white skin of their necks bulge out and in, out and in, out and in real fast. It's the only part of them that moves as they get set to jump back into the grass. When we're through with the frogs, sometimes we become pirates in search of booty. Sometimes we're grieving pet owners at a little spot in the woods where some of Uncle Jack's favorite dogs are buried. Sometimes we'll pretend we're on a picnic in a real picnic area he made—logs placed around a stone-rimmed fire pit. There's space at Uncle Jack's to be anything we want, cowgirls and fishermen, movie stars and everything else we can think of.

Uncle Jack is always on the move, unlike most grown-ups I know who walk around like they've got hundreds of little beanbags sewn under their skin. When we arrive he's always outside, driving his tractor to cut grass in a field, or hauling big branches that have fallen down from the trees into a pile where he saws them apart for fire wood, or he's climbing up a ladder to pick peaches. He's like a kid that way, except he's always working, not playing like we do, and he's pretty serious.

Once he took us on a hayride, and what a fun time we had! He lined the bottom of a wagon with hay and attached it to the back of his tractor and lifted the three of us inside, and we took off—all around the property, three or four times. For us the tractor became six of those big, heavy prancing brown and white horses as we wound around and around acre after acre, through the meadow, into the woods and out near the marsh. So actually, getting to go to Uncle Jack's is another good thing about our move to Hinsdale, one of the nicest.

We've had a lot of weekend visitors since we moved. Each one of them thinks this house and Hinsdale are just peachy. Mommy and Daddy take them on tours around the house, and it's the same thing over and over. The beautiful redwood, the amazing sliding closet doors, the nifty windows that you open by turning a handle instead of sliding up and down, the miraculous folding stairs that pull down from the ceiling. They lead to the attic. Daddy and Mommy both love to demonstrate everything, and I guess it's a nice break from our routine.

We have chores to do here just like we did on Richmond Street. The first thing is making our beds each morning. Absolutely no wrinkles whatsoever allowed. This is really hard for me partly because my mattress is lumpy and partly because I've just never been good at it. Even though I make my bed every day, I never get better at it. The worst part of making our beds though is putting the fitted sheet back on the mattress after it's been washed, which happens every other week. I pull and pull and pull trying to get all the corners down, but just when I think I'm about to get the last corner all tucked over just right, the one kitty-corner from it pops off. I scream and pound my fists on my mattress with all my might each time this happens, and I'm really tired by the time I finally get the sheet on. I hope this will get easier when I get bigger and stronger.

We also set the table for each meal—six of everything for the six of us, plus serving dishes. Then we clear the table when we're done. Sometimes just getting done with a meal is like work. We never leave food on our plates. That's not allowed. Mommy puts a certain amount of each type of food on each of our plates, and we have to eat it all, like it or not. If there's too much food, or if there's something we don't like to eat, we have to sit at the table until we do eat it. Except, she doesn't make me eat mushrooms or fish because Daddy says I don't have to eat them. If one of us is sitting at the table in front of some awful food, and a few hours go by and the food's still not eaten, we get it for the next meal.

One time on Richmond Street, when Daddy was off working on the house here in Hinsdale, I'd eaten everything on my plate. We cleared the dishes, and then Mommy pulled out these things called strawberry tarts. She was smiling, just so happy to be giving us this great treat. It wasn't her cat smile either. She was really making nice. I thought my tart was mighty pretty, but I was so full I couldn't eat it. I just watched everyone eat theirs. Then they all went into the living room to watch the *Lone Ranger* on TV, and I was in the kitchen alone staring at the tart. I wanted to watch the show too, so I slid quiet as a spider out of my chair, lifted my plate up and tip toed over to the garbage can, lifted its lid slowly so it wouldn't squeak, placed my tart gently on top of the garbage, lowered the lid, washed my plate at the sink, dried it, put it on the table because I couldn't reach the cabinet where it was kept, and raced into the living room.

"Did you eat your tart, Laura?" asked Mommy.

"Yes, it's all gone," I said.

"That's impossible. You couldn't have eaten it that fast."

"Yes I did."

"Well, we'll just see about that," Mommy said, getting up from the couch and walking into the kitchen.

I wasn't worried. I never looked inside the garbage can unless I had to put something in there, so I didn't think she would either. But that's the first place she looked. She called me into the kitchen. One of her hands was holding up the lid, the other pointing inside.

"Look in there, Laura, what's that?"

"Uh, I don't know."

"Don't you lie to me. It's your tart, isn't it?"

So I had to fess up. She pulled the tart out of the garbage, put it on the plate I'd just washed and dried, and I had to eat it. Then when I was done, I was in a heap of trouble.

Mommy led me into the bathroom where she had me lean over the sink. She lathered up a bar of soap. Then she held my neck in place with one hand and stuck the bar of soap into my mouth with the other. And she scrubbed my mouth out with me jumping up and down and trying to pull away the whole time. That tasted awful, and I decided while her hand was stuck in my mouth that I have to be extra careful about when and where I lie about something. Then she sent me to bed.

When Daddy got home, she told him what I did, and he belted me. The usual thing, my pants pulled down around my ankles leaning over the bed. Him sliding his belt out of the loops on his pants, and whap, whapping me first for throwing away good food. Even if I hadn't lied about this, it would have been a terrible thing to do. It's a sin to waste food. Then more whap, whaps for lying to Mommy about it.

So now, I always eat everything on my plate no matter how full I am. Once all the food is eaten, Kathy, Mary Ruth and I clear the table. When we have company Mommy's the one who gets the ball rolling by announcing like a circus ringmaster, "And now it's time for my automatic dish washers to go to work." Everybody gets a good laugh from that, except Kathy, Mary Ruth and me.

When it comes to table clearing there's only one way to do it. We stack the dishes—platters, plates and bowls—in separate stacks largest on the bottom, smallest on the top, being sure to scrape any bones onto just one plate so the rest are in a neat stack, easy to carry. And we group the silverware in bunches like flowers. All of this is important so as not to waste a lot of time going back and forth just carrying a random dish or two. That would never, ever do.

Then we put any leftovers from the serving dishes into smaller dishes, cover them with foil, and put them in the refrigerator. Then we wash and dry all the dishes, no matter how burned some of the cooking pans might be. And when Mommy bakes chicken the pan is always burned. It's not okay to let the pan soak for a while to soften up the crud. Whichever one of us is washing that day has to scrape and scrape and scour and scrub until the pan is clean. The other two, the ones on dish drying duty, have to stand and watch too while all this scraping is going on. None of us can leave the kitchen until all the work is done including wiping all the kitchen counters down plus the dining room table. Then one of us scrubs the kitchen sink.

On Saturdays we scour the bathroom sink, clean the toilet, dust all the wooden furniture in the living room and dining room. We vacuum the dining room, living room and hallway, and do other things that just come to Mommy's mind, including practicing piano, which we do every day so it seems like a chore to me, even though I really want to be able to play. We also have to pick up our room every day, and on Saturdays we have to dust it really well too. Usually that's enough when visitors come, except for the O'Neills.

Laura McHale Holland

Something about the O'Neills makes Mommy extra nervous and Daddy a little something else that I can't quite figure out. It's not like he's mad, like when he's about to punish me for something. It's maybe a different sort of mad. So, when we're expecting a visit from the O'Neills, which isn't often, Daddy puts a white glove on his right hand and shows it to us so that we can see how clean it is when he puts it on. Then he starts rubbing surfaces in our room—the molding, Kathy's jewelry box, the cardboard boxes Mommy covered with old wall paper that we keep under our beds that are full of toys and treasures, the pole in the closet, the curtain rod—everything. And it never fails that when he's done, the glove has dust on it, and we have to set to work again.

He doesn't inspect the rest of the rooms with a white glove. Mommy's in charge of those, but she makes us go over everything twice before the O'Neills come, and all the while she mutters things like, "Your Aunt Ruth and Aunt Bea are so tall, they must think I'm a midget, and they have to look down their noses at me" or "The O'Neill's only shop at the best stores, Marshall Field and Carson Pirie Scott, you know. They'd be beside themselves if they knew our table cloth was from Monkey Wards."

Then when the O'Neills arrive, Grampa Adams just shuts himself up in his room, and Mommy always greets Grampa O'Neill with, "Hello Dr. O'Neill, may I take your hat and coat?" Very formal and not at all normal. And things stay like that for the whole visit, like if somebody talks too loud or has a really good belly laugh, something very important will break. Still, it's nice to see them too, and I guess all these visitors are another good thing about living here.

86

Another thing Daddy says is very good about Hinsdale is the education we're going to get here. He complained on Richmond Street about us picking up bad pronunciation in the neighborhood, and at school. One day Kathy said "yous" to him, and he sat all of us down and said, "Yous is not a word, and I don't want to hear it come out of any of your mouths ever again." He's always telling us, "slow down, don't slur your words, " and if we say "can I" instead of "may I" when we want to know if it's okay to do something, he says, "Yes, you can, but I don't know if I'll let you."

He says people in our old neighborhood butcher the English language, and that's a very bad thing to do, and living here is going to nip that in the bud. I heard him tell Grampa O'Neill that we're in one of the best public school systems in the state of Illinois, probably the entire United States of America. That was when Grampa asked him if we were enrolled at St. Isaac Jogues. That's a Catholic school just a little farther away from us than Madison School. Grampa didn't look happy when he learned we were going to public school, and he asked, "What about their religious education?"

Daddy just frowned at this, and then Mommy jumped in, "Oh, we can take care of that with Saturday classes, can't we?"

That was a long time ago, and so far we haven't gone to any Saturday classes to learn about being Catholic. But we have gone a few times to church at St. Isaac Jogues. Its pews are light wood, and it's really bright inside, too bright, I think. It doesn't even feel like the same kind of church I visited with Uncle Rol.

Mommy found some wide, tight, scratchy plastic headbands full of flowers on the top for us all to wear because girls and women have to wear hats in church, and headbands with flowers count as hats. So when we go to church this headband pushes in on my head really hard. Then there is all this standing up, kneeling down, standing up again, kneeling and sitting. Just when I sit down and think all this moving around is over with and I can just relax and stare at the stained glass windows, it's time to kneel again, or stand. It's really uncomfortable. Then there's a time in the mass when all the grown-ups and the bigger kids get to go up and take communion at the altar. That's what Kathy, Mary Ruth and I are going to study for because it's a very bad thing to go up and take communion before you know what it's all about.

I feel more and more disturbed as the mass goes on, mostly because I know we're all supposed to be going to mass at least once a week, and I think that God must be very angry with us for staying away, so my heart starts pounding really hard, and my clothes start to itch. I feel like if I stay there one more minute I'm just going to charge right out of my seat, run screaming down the center aisle up to the priest who's in charge of everything and throw myself at his feet and blurt out, "Save me Father, please, for I am such a wicked girl. My whole family's bad. We hardly ever go to church. My daddy and mommy don't even like the church, and I know we've sinned enough to land in purgatory forever. Please don't spank me for this."

Thank goodness, the whole mess ends before this happens. Once I'm outside I rip off my headband as fast as I can and take in a big gulp of air, and all those feelings I always feel inside the church seem more than silly. They seem like something I couldn't possibly have been feeling.

I don't know what St. Isaac's school would be like, but Madison has been a big let down. I was uncomfortable from the first day I set foot in my classroom. When Mommy brought me to the door everybody else was already sitting down at tables that were just big enough for four students each. The room had bright fluorescent lights that made the whole room seem like every little bit of cozy had been bleached clean away. The teacher and Mommy exchanged a few words, and then the teacher motioned for me to come into the class. "Hello class, this is Laura. She's new to the school," she said.

I stepped through the doorway. Most of the kids glanced up from their tables, but nobody smiled at me. It was an uneasy feeling being looked at that way, like I was being inspected or something. It wasn't like Darwin School where it felt like everybody was my friend. It was creepy—the blank looks on their faces, the way they sat almost like toy soldiers, the complete quiet in the room. The teacher sat me at a table with a dark-skinned girl. She was the only one at the table besides me, and she was trembling. Now I was maybe afraid some, but I wasn't trembling. "This is Donna," the teacher said pointing to the girl next to me, "and I'm Mrs. Claussen."

So I sat there looking at Donna and thought I really need a friend here, and I turned to her and whispered, "Will you be my friend?" and she just changed completely. Her smile was big and wide, and she stopped trembling, and she said, "Yes!" So Donna and I became friends, and for quite a while we were always together in school, like a pair of shoes.

I made friends with Norman a couple days later when we all sat on the floor near the front blackboard so Mrs. Claussen could read us a story. He has a strange way of walking because his right knee doesn't bend, and when he walks, he steps forward with his left foot and then drags the right foot to catch up to the left. When he drag/walked over to a spot near me and plunked down, he accidentally bumped me with his bum leg, and I said, "I feel sorry for you."

"Why?" he said.

"Because your leg is all messed up. Does it hurt?"

"No, I was born this way. It doesn't hurt."

Then he squeezed in close to Donna and me and from then on we were always together—on the swings or the jungle gym or just rolling down the hill on the grass.

I wanted Donna and Norman to come over to play right away, but it took a lot of arranging because Kathy, Mary Ruth and I can only have friends over on Friday. And we have to ask a whole week in advance. I asked way ahead like I'm supposed to do, but Mommy kept putting it off for one reason or other. It was almost the end of October before they finally came to play. The three of us walked the block home from school, and when we came in through the front door Mommy looked us over and told us to play outside.

Well, the sun was shining. It wasn't summer hot, but it was nice and warm. So we were okay outside playing with my plastic farm animals on our scraggly lawn for a while. Pretty soon Donna's mom and Norman's mom came to pick each of them up, saying a quick thank you to Mommy at the door. Then I was inside practicing the piano. It was almost like they'd never come to visit at all.

Later on I heard Mommy talking and laughing on the phone, not just to her friend Florence, who she complains to just about every day, but to three or four different people,

"Can you believe it? Laura brought home a little Negro girl, yessiree a Negro girl. And that's not all. Oh, no, she brought home a cripple boy too. Yeah, he's got one leg so stiff all he can do is drag it. Doesn't that just take the cake? Of all the kids in her class, these are the ones she goes for. Yeah, now I really know there's something wrong with her. This is proof positive."

Pretty soon after that Norman decided he loved me in this really strange way. He started chasing me around the playground trying to get me caught up against the school building so he could kiss me. I could outrun him because of his bum leg, but I felt really disgusted because Norman was my friend and all, but I didn't want to kiss him. I didn't want to kiss anybody. Then he asked me to marry him, and I said, "No, no, never!" because I was thinking I don't want to get married, and if I ever do, it will probably be to Charlie. But Norman didn't stop. He kept asking and chasing and saying that he loved me. Donna and I kept telling him to leave me alone. But he followed us everywhere we went, like gum stuck to the soles of our shoes.

None of the other kids paid any attention. It was just Donna and me on our own against Norman. I didn't much like the way Donna, Norman and I were always together, never playing with other kids, but it didn't really start to bother me until Norman got this crazy kissing thing stuck in his head. Then I started to notice that whenever Donna and Norman and I came up, other kids didn't notice us, no matter how much we tried to get their attention. They'd go off to another part of the playground or huddle with their backs close together. It's not like they said anything mean or even told us to go away. They just closed us out.

Kids did whisper strange things to me in line though, things I just ignored until Norman went off the deep end with his love thing. "Haven't you noticed how stupid Norman is? Everybody knows he's retarded," a girl named Lindsey whispered to me when we were in the back of the classroom putting some watercolor pictures we'd just painted on a table to dry.

Then a boy named Andy started standing behind me when we lined up for recess. The first time he asked me, "Do you know what everybody's calling you?"

"No," I said.

"They're calling you monkey lover, monkey lover," he said, pointing to Donna and pretending to scratch his armpits and then making ooh, ooh sounds sort of like The Three Stooges might make. After that I never knew when he was going to sneak up behind me and call me monkey lover and make those awful noises, and if I happened to look his way during class he would do the armpit thing. It made me feel really creepy and choked up.

Then one day he got behind Donna in line and sniffed real deep at her neck, right where her snow-white collar met her deep brown skin. He made an ugly face like he'd just eaten raw oysters or something, and whispered to me, "Something wrong with your nose? She smells different, really bad different. How can you stand it? Can't you smell?"

After that when I stood next to Donna, which was just about all the time at school, I would find myself thinking that she really did smell different. The thoughts just drifted in, like a swarm of gnats in the summer. I tried not to pay attention, but the thoughts just kept flying in big as you please whenever they wanted to. Everything Donna did started to bug me, her smile, her soft voice, her long legs. I wanted to get away from her. I wanted to stop this buzzing line of thinking and feeling, but I couldn't.

Kids kept on saying stuff—not every day, but often enough so I couldn't forget that something was not right about my friends and me. The other kids were never loud. They never teased me or hit me the way Kathy and Mary Ruth do when they're not happy with me. It was always a quiet thing, a quick tap on my shoulder, a little whisper in my ear that nobody else could hear.

Then one day Norman told Mrs. Claussen that he and I were getting married the very next day. She said, "Why Norman, that's wonderful," and she announced to the class, "Everybody, Laura and Norman are getting married tomorrow." All the kids except Donna looked at me like I was suddenly cross-eyed. I hoped the whole thing would just go away. But the next day when I came into the classroom, there was Norman holding a veil he made from an Oscar Mayer wiener wrapper to go around my head and toilet paper stapled on for a veil, and a ring he'd made from a the foil part of a gum wrapper. I nearly fainted right there on the classroom floor. Then Mrs. Claussen got the whole class in a circle. She had Norman and me stand up in front of the group. Norman put the veil on me, and the ring. I was standing there feeling like my old Bozo the Clown punching toy that is all deflated down in our basement. Bozo has a hole in his plastic bottom that even Daddy can't fix. Then Mrs. Claussen said, "There now. Laura and Norman are married."

Everyone just stared quietly, and I could tell I was red in the face because my cheeks felt like they'd been slapped. When I got back to my table, I took off the veil and ring, and stuffed them underneath in this little cubbyhole thing that's part of the table. Then at recess I took the veil and ring to the trash can, ripped them up right there in front of Norman and squished them down real good. I said, "I don't want to marry you, and I don't want to be your friend anymore either." He finally got the message. He and I haven't spoken since.

Then for a while it was Norman all by himself at recess, usually picking at little holes in the brick of the school building, me playing with Donna, and all the other kids playing in their little groups that slipped and slid away from us like mercury that had escaped from a broken thermometer. Then one day as we were lining up to go to morning recess Jillie stood behind me in line, pointed to Donna who was right in front of me and whispered in my ear, "Lots of kids would want to be your friend if you stop being friends with her."

"Really? Who?" I asked.

"I would. I could even come over and play with you after school today."

"Oh, I can't play today."

"Why not?"

"I can only play on Fridays, and I have to ask a week ahead of time, and then most of the time it's still not okay."

"Wow. That's weird."

I thought about what Jillie had said, and I thought about all the other things kids had whispered to me about Donna. It struck me that as long as I was her friend I wasn't going to be friends with anybody else, except maybe Norman, but I didn't want to be his friend anymore. Then I did a really bad thing. I decided to dump Donna. It took me a couple weeks of trying until I could squish my heart to a place where I could ignore Donna like everybody else.

Then one day right after morning recess Mrs. Claussen called us all up to the front of the room so we could sit close together on the floor and listen to her tell us about how in 1492 Columbus sailed the ocean blue all the way to America. She had three small wooden ships with fancy sails on her lap, which she said were just like the real ships he used. Donna and I were right next to each other, as usual. I decided then and there it was the time to act. I turned to her and said, "I don't want to be your friend anymore."

I crawled away from her even though it was hard to do because I felt physically drawn to her like a magnet. She crawled after me, smiling wide, thinking it was a game, but I said it again, " I don't want to be your friend anymore." And I added, "It's the truth."

I crawled away again and she followed me. Then after we did this about five times, Mrs. Claussen told us to stop moving around. And she said to Donna, who was on the other side of the group from me, "Stay where you are. You can see she doesn't want to sit next to you, can't you?"

So Donna sat where she was, tears welling in her eyes as other kids near her shifted away just a little bit, and I tried not to look at her as I sat alone too, still as a fox about to pounce on a bird, afraid that if I moved one muscle I'd look over at Donna, and I didn't want to risk facing her big, sad brown eyes.

After school I raced home and asked Mommy if I could have Jillie over. She said it would be okay not for the next Friday, but for the one after that. When the day finally came, Jillie walked home with me. We were just sitting down with my toy cars to get some sort of game going, when the doorbell rang. It was Jillie's mom. She said, "Is Jillie here?"

"Why yes, she is," Mommy said standing in the doorway.

"I'm so glad. Mrs. Claussen said she thought she saw the girls walking away from school together."

"Didn't you know she was coming over?"

"No, I didn't."

By this point Jillie and I were standing near the door, trying to figure out if one or both of us was in trouble over this.

"I'd love for Jillie to come play with Laura sometime, but today's not a good day. She has a doctor's appointment this afternoon. I'm so sorry. How about tomorrow?"

"Tomorrow won't do. Laura has work to do."

"Okay, how about Monday?"

"No, Laura has to practice piano."

"Tuesday?"

"Not Tuesday, she has piano practice then too."

"Does she practice every afternoon?"

I wanted Mommy to say, "How about next Friday?" But she didn't. She said that I do practice every day. Jillie's mom said, "Well, okay then, maybe another time. Come on, Jillie. Let's go."

Jillie slipped out the door and walked away with her mom. I haven't asked her to come back, and she hasn't asked me over to her house either. She told me her best friend, Diane, hates me and doesn't want her to play with me. Diane thinks I'm a show off because of that wedding thing with Norman. Jillie also said that her mommy said that my mommy's strange. I told her I know that, and she giggled, but I just turned away.

Since then I haven't played with anybody except Kathy and Mary Ruth after school. All the rigamarole we have to go through to get together with classmates is too much of a bother for them. Mommy likes it that way. She says we have each other and that's all we need, and other people will probably just give us diseases anyway. Sometimes we play outside with other kids on the block, like Walter and Bonnie next door and the Reid kids on the other side, but we aren't allowed to ask any of them inside, and we're never invited inside their homes either.

Being at school's gotten a little better though. Everybody got really excited when the locusts came just a few weeks ago. It was such a big event that I felt more a part of the group in an odd way. We all couldn't stop talking about them and examining them at recess. Even the teachers and our parents were all caught up in it. First there were just a few of these plump flying insects about an inch long with beady bulging eyes, wings so strong and fast that they buzz, and legs that wiggle and wiggle when you pick them up. It was okay to pick them up because they didn't bite. They crawled out of their skins and left them behind on the ground everywhere like some sort of discarded light brown armor. Then they went for the trees and bushes and started to eat, eat, eat the leaves.

More and more of them came, leaving their little skin armors on the ground so that in some places the ground was completely covered by them and we crunched on them when we walked to school. They buzzed and buzzed all day long. The sound went on and on and on. Mrs. Claussen said it was the sound of their wings flapping. They stripped the leaves completely from some trees and bushes. In our yard the worst thing they did was eat off one entire branch of our little apple tree that was supposed to produce five different kinds of apples. It started out with one kind, but four branches of different types of apples had been grafted to its trunk. Now it's just got four kinds of apples. But it survived.

One Saturday during the locust invasion Daddy took me to downtown Hinsdale to do some errands. It was a treat being with him and a treat going to town. Mommy always does her shopping out of town. She says Hinsdale's way too expensive. On the ride downtown he asked me, "So how do you like the locusts?"

"They're okay, kind of exciting."

"Noisy though, aren't they."

"Yeah, and I'm mad at them for hurting our apple tree."

We rode on a block or two in silence. Then he asked, "Why do you suppose they call them the seventeen-year locusts?" He thought he had me stumped, I'm sure, but Mrs. Claussen had just told us about that, so I said, "Because they come only once every seventeen years."

"That's right," he said. We smiled at each other. I was relieved. But then he asked, "How old will you be when they come again?"

This made me shrink down into my seat so that I could barely see the world outside the car windows. I knew I had to answer and answer pretty fast so as not to make him angry with me. But if my answer was wrong he'd be angry for that too. I counted up six from seventeen, even though everybody says it's cheating to just count up to add, and I blurted out, "Twenty-three."

Daddy smiled. "What do you think you'll be doing when you're twenty-three?"

"Maybe I'll be a mom," I said.

"Maybe."

"What do you think you'll be doing?"

"Probably still working hard to pay off your college bills."

We drove on in silence, and I got to thinking about how far, far into the future being twenty-three is. It doesn't seem possible that I'll ever be twenty-three, just like it doesn't seem possible that Mommy or Daddy or Gramma ever were children even though they say they were young a long time ago. I wonder if they had friends to play with at school.

Now at recess I run over to the swings and fly through the air by myself. I'm usually one of the first ones there so I rarely have to wait for a turn. Every now and then I stay on one swing the whole time. Sometimes I slide down the slide or climb on the jungle gym, but I'm usually alone if I do. It seems all the groups of friends formed at the beginning of the year, and there isn't really any group that wants me to join. Sometimes they'll let me be part of a game when it's more fun to have a lot of players, like in hide-and-seek, or tag. But I have to ask to be part of something.

I wish Daddy would announce that it was a big mistake to move here and that we're going back to Richmond Street just as soon as we can get everything packed up. But I don't think that's going to happen, so I'm hoping that next year when I'm in a new class with a new teacher I'll be able to make some friends I can keep.

Hank caught many a girl's eye, with his Clark Gable magnetism and angular features like Gregory Peck. And he was smitten with me, of all people. I was curious, for I was never the one who made the boys' hearts fly. Yet to Hank I was a princess, a dream, everything he'd ever wanted. I was fragrant and gentle, with soft manicured hands, but I could work chemistry problems as well as he could.

He joked about our teachers, teased me, and spoke of God in irreverent terms. But at least he was Catholic. His love notes came on ripped school paper, mine on Hummel cards. My friends were cordial, but not approving, my family patronizing. They all expected he would go away, that I would recover from him as though from the flu. So did I.

Mary Agnes

Wishes

School is like getting stale bread for every meal, every day, until the very last day, which is all berries and whipped cream. And the last day of fourth grade is finally here. I'm not one of those kids who gets bored during the summer. Put me outside in the sunshine with nothing to do, and I'll be happy to watch grasshoppers chew their cud or hummingbirds flit by the salvia in our front yard. Anything is better than being stuck for hours in one of these desks, being quiet, looking at the blackboard and dreading Miss Dixon's glare, because her discipline is to fourth graders what Kryptonite is to Superman. I guess you could say I hate school. Whenever somebody asks me what my favorite part of the school day is, my answer is always recess. And summer vacation is like one long recess, at least when I'm outside, which is most the time because Mommy doesn't want Kathy, Mary Ruth and me inside unless we're practicing the piano or doing housework.

On the last day of school, we can wear whatever we want, so every last one of us is wearing shorts. And the only thing we're really here to do is pick up our report cards, which won't take long. But just now Miss Dixon did a little something extra, something really nice. Before she passed out our report cards, she passed out some prizes. She gave two of them to me. One was a thick pad of blank white paper for doing well in spelling, and the other was a set of twenty-four beautiful colored pencils for being the only student to not miss any days of school. I can't say that I deserved any credit for my attendance. Mommy sends me to school sick or well. But it's such a surprise to have the colored pencils, especially from Mrs. Dixon who is pretty scary.

The first day of school she told us to write a page about what we did over summer vacation. She gave us a long time in class to work on it. Then we each passed our pencil-scribbled blue ruled paper up to the front of the class. She sat in a chair at the front of the room, holding the pile in front of her and squinting through her thick glasses as she read over our work. Every so often she'd pull out a really bad paper and read part of it out loud, not the way the kid who wrote it meant it to be, but the way it really sounded with all the spelling mistakes.

When she'd gotten through the whole stack, she held up the one she thought was the worst. It began like this, "This summer I hade a fin tim with my momy and dady." Then she called up this boy named Dennis to the front of the class. His whole face was red, his ears were red, even his neck was red. She handed the paper back to him and asked, "Are you sure you belong in fourth grade?" After that I think just about everybody in class slouched down a bit into our desks, hoping, praying that she wouldn't go on with this. I thought if she read my paper, it would have tons of mistakes too, and I might run to the window and jump out. Then I'd end up like the little birds that fall out of their nests tucked in just below the roof. It happens in springtime and the sidewalk is littered with limp bird bodies—gray, tiny and completely without feathers.

I used to think that if I picked the babies up and cared for them, they'd get better, but nobody recovers from death. It's a forever thing. And for a few steps way back in second grade, I held forever in my hands until my teacher that year, Mrs. Paxton, told me to throw the baby bird in the trash and wash my hands, said the baby bird was unsanitary, could make me sick, said I should never pick one up again.

"But I want to make it better," I said.

"You can't, honey. You can't. It's dead," she said. "Dead means it'll never open its eyes again; it'll never breathe again. It's gone, even though the body's here. That body's going to rot soon. Can't you tell there's something important missing?"

She was nice that way, Mrs. Paxton. Explaining things, like death. I wish she'd been my teacher for third and fourth grades too, but that's not how school works. You have a different teacher every year. Mrs. Paxton had a nose like an upside-down mushroom, but she was really kind. But not even she, who could get me to grasp something mysterious like death, could get me to like arithmetic.

For practice she put up different flash cards on her closet door. It was at the front of the class and to the right. There were about twenty problems in addition and subtraction. Numbers bother me. They remind me of the notes on the page when I practice piano. I know there's a connection between the lines and spaces and the notes and rests and clefs and all the other stuff on the page and what I'm supposed to be playing on the keyboard with my fingers. The music paper is there for a reason. I know that. But when I look at the page, it seems like the notes are doing somersaults across the page.

I started pretending to do my arithmetic problems in class and then saying I couldn't find my paper the next day when Mrs. Paxton wanted to collect them. My desk was such a mess, she believed me for a while. I honestly don't know how other kids manage to have all their supplies and papers put away and stacked neatly. It seems impossible to me. I was ashamed of my desk until I started pretending to lose my arithmetic papers. Then it came in handy. But after a while, Mrs. Paxton got wise to me. She started asking me for my paper right at the end of our arithmetic time, and that ended my fooling her.

Brad sat in front of me for a while in Mrs. Paxton's class, and he was really good at arithmetic. I thought maybe he and I would be friends when he moved into a great big house on our block. I guess I expected he'd like me as much as Charlie from Richmond Street did. It didn't happen. Brad has lived in Hinsdale since he was born. Both of his parents grew up here too. He has lots of friends, and he sure doesn't need me. So I was really surprised and happy that when his birthday rolled around he invited me to his party.

I wore a beautiful red dress, one that Aunt Ruth O'Neill took me shopping to buy at Marshall Field & Company. Mommy never takes me clothes shopping or shoe shopping. Most of my dresses are hand-me-downs from Kathy. Mommy says Mary Ruth's dresses are so wide they'll never fit me. Now, as far as Mary Ruth being wide, I think it's like one of those riddles Daddy likes to stump us with at the supper table. He'll ask, "Which came first, the chicken or the egg?"

Mary Ruth is kind of wide, but Mommy also always gives her more food than she gives to Kathy and me. As she loads scoop after scoop of whatever casserole we're having onto Mary Ruth's plate she says, "Here, Mary Ruth, you're a big pig. Eat this." We have to eat everything on our plates, so maybe that's what came first, the mound of food to eat, not the fat. I don't know.

I don't know where Mommy gets our clothes either, but most of them are used even before Kathy gets them. So when the O'Neills buy us something new on our birthdays and at Christmas, it's a real treat. After we've opened our presents though, Mommy stuffs them back in their boxes right away and stores them on a shelf in our hall closet, way behind a tall stack of sheets. We don't even try our outfits on. She pulls them out only for special occasions. Some clothes are packed away for years waiting for the right occasion. Often we've already outgrown them before Mommy takes them out. One Christmas she even gave her cousin Muriel's daughter a beautiful purple sweater and skirt set the O'Neills had given me for my birthday just a few months before. She probably thought I'd forgotten all about it, but I remember every single outfit they've given me. So, I was thrilled when she pulled out such a pretty dress for the party. I practically pranced over to Brad's house.

We played lots of games at the party. One of them was a three-legged race where you had one of your ankles tied to another kid's ankle, and you had to race from one spot to another all over the house, even up and down stairs. I was paired up with Clare because we were around the same size. But I guess I moved too fast and started to drag her around.

I was telling her, "Hurry up, Clare."

But she was hanging back, telling me, "Slow down, Laura."

I didn't want to slow down, and I thought if I kept urging her she'd get some energy and start moving, but the harder I tried to get us moving, the more she shrank back. And then she started screeching, "Laura, stop, stop!"

But I didn't pay attention because first of all it was a race, and just about everybody was making some sort of noise, and second of all because Kathy, Mary Ruth and I screech and scream at each other to stop what we're doing all the time, and none of us ever stops just because of that. We only stop what we're doing to each other if it gets real serious, like there's blood spurting from one of our noses or something. I mean if Clare had even fallen down, I would have stopped, but she was just hanging back, and I was trying to get her to move faster. We were in a race, after all, and the way Kathy, Mary Ruth and I play, it's no big deal to get a little scratched up if you're likely to win something.

But when the race was over, and Brad's mom untied our ankles, Clare started to cry. She peeled her lace-fringed party sock from her ankle and said, "Look what Laura did to me."

Everyone could see that she had a rope burn, and she thought it was a big deal. Well, I had a rope burn too, but to me it was nothing. I've had them before from playing really hard, like on tug of war. But you should have seen the look Brad's mom gave me as she put her arm around Clare and led her away. It was like I was a giant pile of barf.

At school the next Monday I got a little report from Jillie. She wasn't even at the party, but somehow she found out everything that went on. She said everybody was whispering about how I'd gotten wild at the party, and I was in big trouble now with Clare and Brad and their moms.

Sometimes I look out our dining room window and see kids from school going up Brad's front stairs. I guess I really am too wild to be included. I blew my chance to be his friend. He hardly ever even looks outside as far as I can tell. His sister Debbie never comes out of their yard either. I see her by herself dancing in the grass, twirling around in costumes, but never looking our way.

It seems that all of the girls on our block stay inside most of the time except for Kathy, Mary Ruth and me. They sew and cook and do other girl stuff. We're not allowed to do that kind of thing though. Inside we do all the cleaning and scrubbing, and if we want, we can stand by the stove and watch Mommy cook, or sit at her knees in the living room and watch her sew a hem, but she says we'd make too much of a mess if she allowed us to cook or sew something ourselves. Kathy and Mary Ruth have both argued saying, "We do the clean up anyway. Why can't we clean up after ourselves?" But her answer is always a big fat no.

We're not like girls in other ways too because we don't play with dolls, roller skate, or jump rope. As far as roller skating goes, it's not easy to learn how to do it on a gravel driveway and gravel street like ours with one pair of metal slip-over-your-shoes, adjustable skates for the three of us to share. We tried once taking the skates to the school grounds where there's the sidewalk and a bit of pavement too, but we fell down a lot and didn't like having to keep taking them on and off and passing them around.

Jumping rope is something we could do. We have a nice long one that Unc gave Mary Ruth for her last birthday. But that takes something called cooperation, and cooperation doesn't come naturally to us at all. No matter what we're doing it's two against one, and which two of us are banded together against the third changes several times a day, depending upon what's going on.

Now with jump rope it's always the two rope turners against the jumper. Rope turning gets boring really fast, and so the two turners start itching right away to make it more interesting. First thing we usually do is mess with the rhythm, sometimes going extra slow then speeding up and then slowing down again in an unpredictable way. If the jumper lasts through that, we ripple the rope as we turn it, and then if the jumper still hasn't missed, we'll just all of a sudden pull the rope taut so it's more like a parallel bar than a rope. All of this makes it impossible for the jumper to last long.

We usually end up so mad at each other, we have to stop and get away from each other before we start socking and biting. Daddy started belting all three of us if even just two of us get caught fighting, even if the third one isn't in the same room when the fight breaks out. This seems hugely unfair to us, but it does keep us from fighting as much, which, I guess, is the point.

During recess at school when girls are turning ropes real nice for each other and everyone around is chanting a jump rope ditty about B52 airplanes, the jumpers do wonderful things. They jump in and out of the rope while it's still turning; they jump around to face in different directions all the while never hitting the rope; they jump two at a time; they hit the heels of their shoes with their hands when they're in the air, and I chant along, watching in amazement. I never ask to join in. I know I'd just clomp on the rope first thing and make a big fool of myself. I have a way of doing that. I really stuck my foot in it the first day of school in third grade, and I've been extra careful about what I do and say at school ever since.

The summer before third grade, I was walking from our bedroom to the kitchen and liking the soft sunlight coming in through the screen door, landing in sprinkles on the floor. I was hoping I'd find some chocolate cupcakes in the kitchen for breakfast. We used to have cereal and bowls to match different brands of cereal that Mommy had gotten at some supermarket promotion. Mine was light blue and had bears that went with the Sugar Pops cereal, so every morning I had to eat Sugar Pops. I hated them. Mary Ruth got to eat corn flakes. Kathy got Cheerios. One day Kathy complained about us always having to eat the cereal that matched the figures on our bowls, and Mommy said, "So, you don't like cereal now. Is that it?"

"No, no," Kathy replied, "We just don't want to eat the kind that matches our bowls all the time."

"Well alrighty then, girls, if you don't like cereal, you'll have cake instead. How's that?"

This was, I think, supposed to be a punishment, and sometimes if she makes coffee cake with nuts and fruit that looks like it's from the inside of a fish, it is. But usually it's chocolate cake and cupcakes we get from the Burney Brothers outlet that sells leftover stuff from the day before. Day-old anything doesn't fit into Hinsdale, so we have to drive a long way to get them. But Kathy, Mary Ruth and I are happy to ride along to pick up the goodies. Eating chocolate in the morning is the last thing I think of as a punishment.

So there I am in the hallway enjoying sweet summer freedom before the start of third grade. I'm picturing myself biting into one of those cupcakes—they have the fluffiest, sweetest whipped cream in the center—and I hear Mommy giving Kathy and Mary Ruth what for.

"I can't really blame Laura. She was too young to know any better, but you two, you two, you two were so intolerable, you drove your mother, your very own mother, Mary Agnes, to hang herself. Yes indeed, she committed suicide, just up and killed herself, because she couldn't take it anymore with you, but you're not going to do the same thing to me. I won't let you. You've made all of the O'Neills and your father suffer. Oh, how they've all suffered because of you, but not me. Do you hear me? You're not going to get me like you got her!"

I freeze there in the sunlight and take a deep breath as her words sink in. Right off the bat I know it isn't true about me being too young. Whatever it is, if Kathy and Mary Ruth are responsible for something bad, I know I am too. I feel so strange. It seems like all of the floating dust particles in the shafts of sunlight are suddenly vibrating wildly.

And then I remember a time on Richmond Street when Kathy and Mary Ruth were both in school, but I hadn't started kindergarten yet. Mommy and I were having lunch in the kitchen. I had just learned the story of Cinderella. I was thinking about how awful her stepmother was to make her work all the time and not let her go to the ball. I said to Mommy, "Stepmothers are really mean."

She looked at me and she looked like I imagine Captain

Hook would look if he didn't have his mustache. She said, "I'm your stepmother, so I suppose you think I'm mean then, don't you?"

I was very confused. I didn't know what to say. I just took a bite of my butter and sugar sandwich and smiled as I chewed. I thought she was playing some kind of trick on me. I was trying to figure out what it was.

"Okay, since you're not talking, you really must think I'm a mean old stepmother. So little miss dissatisfied, you can just find another place to live."

She left the kitchen and came back with a little gray suitcase and said, "Here I've even packed your bag for you. If I were so mean I'd have made you do it yourself. Now get off that chair."

"That's not mine," I said, scowling at the suitcase. "Mine's red and sparkly."

"That broken down old thing? I threw it out ages ago."

She yanked me by the wrist and pulled me to the front door, opened it, pushed me through, and put the suitcase beside me.

"Goodbye," she said, and slammed the door.

I sat there, stunned, but not altogether unhappy. I thought I'd really rather live at Gramma's anyway. I picked up the suitcase. It wasn't as heavy as I thought it would be. I clomped down the stairs and on to the sidewalk, suitcase bouncing along beside me. I thought maybe if I just started walking I'd figure out how to get to Gramma's. Charlie's mom was outside planting flowers in her front yard. She asked me what I was doing. "I'm going to my gramma's," I said. Then Mommy grabbed me from behind and said to Charlie's mom,

111

"Honestly, this child has such a wild imagination, always dreaming up fantasy games." She and Charlie's mom both laughed. Then Mommy picked up the suitcase and told me to follow her as she limped on back to our house.

I'd always thought Mommy was just being goofy that day when she said she was my stepmother. But as I stand there in the hallway, thinking over all the nasty stuff she'd just said to Kathy and Mary Ruth, the idea that someone who was my mother had killed herself long ago sounds more and more real to me. But I am trying to figure out why Daddy said Mommy is my mother if she really isn't. He seemed so sure of it when he told me that day I arrived on Richmond Street, and he's always right. He just is. I want to stay in the hallway for a while and try to figure all of this out, but I know if I don't show up at the kitchen counter soon Mommy will come looking for me. I take a deep breath, walk into the kitchen and grab a chocolate cupcake.

"Good morning," I say. I pull the moist paper from the cupcake and lick off some of the frosting.

"Yeah right," Kathy says under her breath, "Laura was too young. It wasn't her fault."

"What's not my fault?" I say. I take a bite out of the cupcake.

"Watch it, Katherine, or I'll tell your father. And you, Laura, pipe down and eat your breakfast." Back to Kathy she says, "Don't get into a fight first thing in the morning, Miss Royal Highness, or you're going to spend the summer working your fingers to the bone."

Kathy and Mary Ruth glare at me, and I glare right back. We polish off the whole pack of cupcakes in silence before we each go our separate ways outside in the yard. I plop down on some crabgrass and watch bumblebees buzz all around the sweet pea blossoms by our basement window. I think of Mommy's words and of other things I've heard over the years, and I start to put things together in a new way, the way they were supposed to be, the way everybody else in my family probably knew they were all along.

It finally makes sense why Mommy calls Grampa O'Neill Doctor instead of Dad. I get it. He never was her father. He was Mary Agnes's father, and Mary Agnes was this mother I had who killed herself. I remember a picture of her on Grampa O'Neill's dresser, a dark haired woman in a white blouse, her eyes looking far off and dreamy, and I try to feel some feelings for Mary Agnes. I close my eyes and stretch out flat and think really hard about her, but nothing comes. I feel more about the robin hopping around, looking for worms at the other side of the yard than I do about this Mary Agnes person. Maybe Kathy, Mary Ruth and I were so bad she didn't want to be ours anymore. Now only the O'Neills get to feel anything about her. She belongs to them, not us. That must be what happens when you're really bad.

Later that summer Kathy, Mary Ruth and I are playing hide-and-seek at the Rusa's in Downers Grove. I am hidden in some bushes near the back of Uncle Jack's toolshed. Uncle Jack and Grampa Adams walk toward me and stop by a peach tree maybe six feet away. Uncle Jack jabs the end of his shovel down in the dirt, puts both hands on the handle and leans toward Grampa Adams. He looks angry when he says, "Why do you have to keep bringing them here? We're too old to have kids running around the place anymore."

"Ahh, what about your ehh grandkids. They ehh come 'round."

"That's different. They're older, and they're family."

I back away quietly, not wanting to hear any more, but I trip on a tree stump sticking up only an inch or so from the ground. I fall with a big thud. They both look over and for a second my eyes meet theirs. Then I get up and run away as fast as I can.

When Mommy calls us into Uncle Jack's house for a snack, I walk in slow as a mule and study each one of those grown-ups—Mommy, Grampa Adams, Uncle Jack, Aunt Dorothy, and their daughter Violet. I decide while eating my slice of crunchy-topped bread that I don't care about these people anyway. I don't want to be with anybody who doesn't want to be with me. I'm not theirs and they're not mine. And if Uncle Jack ever asks me if I wanted to go on a hayride again, I'll say a great big NO, even though they are an awful lot of fun. But I am still going to enjoy playing in the woods with Kathy and Mary Ruth. Uncle Jack isn't going to take that away. Out there I can forget that he exists.

Ever since then, even more things began to make sense. Mommy always frets on the way over to Downers Grove, thinking out loud about whether she should have brought four dozen eggs instead of three dozen, whether the cherries she brought are ripe enough, whether she stayed too long last time we came. It's like this stuff is her ticket in, but no matter what she brings, she's only allowed to stay a certain amount of time. I learned why she says Uncle Jack's daughters aren't really her cousins, too. Grampa Adams wasn't always her father. He used to be her uncle, and he was married to Uncle

Jack's sister, who was her aunt. She never knew her daddy, and her mommy died in a big flu epidemic before she even started school. That's when her aunt and uncle adopted her.

Mommy just started talking about her past one afternoon when we were in the kitchen pulling hard little peas from their pods. She said that her real daddy died when she was so small she doesn't remember him, and then Mommy's real mommy married again. Her mommy and stepdad had another child, a boy, and they all moved to a farm in Wisconsin, the place that makes Mommy feel so bad to talk about. Then there was a big flu epidemic, and Mommy's mommy died. Mommy's stepfather dumped her in an orphanage in Chicago and went back to someplace in Europe where he'd come from. He took his son along and ditched Mommy. While she was in the orphanage Mommy got scarlet fever and her left eardrum got punctured, and so she can't hear out of that ear. Grampa Adams found out she was there, took her out, and adopted her. So that's how Grampa Adams and his wife went from being her aunt and uncle to her mom and dad. I guess that wasn't good enough for the Rusas because she's not related to them by blood, and Mommy says that's important, and Kathy, Mary Ruth and I are even less related because we're not related to them or even to Mommy by blood.

I asked Mommy if the scarlet fever at the orphanage had anything to do with her limp and her back hurting so much of the time, so that she's always rubbing it with the back of her hand. And I asked about her elbows too. They itch so much that she scratches them raw, and she has to wear these little bandage things she makes out of old T-shirts, and sometimes old socks, to protect herself from her scratching. I guess that was going too far on my part. She didn't want to talk anymore about the past. She said, "Oh, little miss buddinsky, wouldn't you just like to know. You probably think I'm some kind of freak. Well, this isn't a freak show, dearie. Mind your own beeswax." And then she clammed up.

By the end of the summer I decided the only people I know for sure I belong to are Kathy, Mary Ruth, Daddy, Gramma and Unc. Everybody else belongs more to somebody else than to me. The O'Neills all belong together. Mommy and Grampa Adams belong together. The Rusas belong together. I don't belong to any of them. But I kept mum about all of this stuff until the first day of third grade when I made a stupid mess of things in the washroom with Lizzie.

I don't know Lizzie at all. The only time I've ever talked to her is that day in the bathroom. Kids say she's an oddball because she always wears brown, every single day, and she talks real soft. Since nobody pays much attention to her, maybe I thought she would be an okay person to tell something I'm not supposed to tell anybody about. It's not that I can remember anybody telling me not to say anything. It's just that when I think about telling somebody about Mary Agnes, it feels just like when I've dropped one of our dishes by accident and watched it break apart and scatter across the kitchen tile, knowing I would get belted for it no matter how much I apologized. But I wanted to try talking about Mary Agnes anyway. So there in the girls' bathroom I was washing my hands like you're supposed to do after you pee. Lizzie was still in her stall, probably doing number two. It was while I lathered up my hands that it popped into my head that I could tell Lizzie about my mother not really being my mother and see what happened.

I stood there at the sink looking at the soap bubbles multiply on my hands. She came out of her stall and stood at the sink next to me. As water ran over her hands I thought now, now, tell her now, but I couldn't make a noise. I started rinsing my hands as she spurted pink liquid soap from the dispenser on her hands and began to rub them together above the sink, making lather. My hands were all rinsed, but I keep holding them under the water, moving them around as though there were still traces of lather on my skin. Then she rinsed her hands real quick, pulled them out from under the faucet, and reached for a paper towel. I turned off the faucet, and I reached for a paper towel too. In that moment as we stood facing each other, brown paper getting soggy as we wiped our hands dry, I looked into her big blue eyes peeking out from her long blond bangs and I said, "You know my mother isn't really my mother." It felt as I said this as though I was trying to pry off a lid to a jar that I just wasn't strong enough to master.

Lizzie said, "Oh, yeah? Well, who is she then?"

I said, "I don't know who she is, but she's not my mommy. My mommy committed suicide." The word sounded like a wrong note when I'm practicing piano.

"What's suicide?" Lizzie asked.

And I said, "Suicide is when you kill yourself. My mommy killed herself." My throat was all of a sudden dry and scratchy and the walls of the washroom seemed to be closing in on me.

Lizzie looked at me, her eyes wide like she'd just stepped into a horror movie or something, and she said, "That's not nice, Laura. You're mean to say that to me. I don't believe you either. You're a liar, liar pants on fire."

Feeling dizzy, I leaned against the sink. I'd been expecting something different, hoping to feel something, something new and better, but instead I felt like I'd been squished into a glass tube that was pressing in on all sides so I was having trouble breathing. I wanted Lizzie to say something that would magically pull me out of the tube, but she stuck her tongue out at me, turned around and ran out of the bathroom. I leaned on the sink and stared into the mirror. At least I didn't look squished. I promised myself then and there never to mention my real mother again to anyone. Then I felt a little bit better.

I knew by the way Lizzie and the kids sitting near her looked at me when I walked back into the classroom that she had told them what I'd said. And that's when I knew I'd made a big fool of myself. My only hope as I sat down at my desk was that since it was Lizzie, the baby, doing the talking, nobody would believe her. Nobody's ever asked me about it, and I try to just keep my mind on what the teachers tell me to do so I don't go blabbing like that again. That worked out pretty well in third grade. My teacher, Mrs. Flynn, gave me the best grades I've ever gotten on my report cards. Mommy said it was because she was about to retire and didn't have all of her marbles and that no good teacher could possible give me such high marks.

Miss Dixon hasn't been as easy on me as Mrs. Flynn, but my grades have been okay, and now I have these pencils she gave me in my hand, which makes me think maybe she's not as bad as I thought. I'm going to draw lots of pictures with them this summer while I sit in the grass, blue sky overhead, the smell of flowers in the wind, sun on my face, and all the time in the world to feel the heat soak in.

I got a bigger surprise than pencils this year though. I was longing for a pair of saddle shoes and a soft gray skirt with a pink poodle on the front, a pink sweater with sleeves that end just above my elbows, a pair of tights—any color would do—and for Mommy to say it's okay for me to grow my hair into a ponytail. Then I could look more like the other girls in school. Grampa Adams had just cut my hair by putting a bowl on my head and snipping around the edges, so I was looking even stranger than usual. Maybe that's what got me going. I'm usually pretty good about not wanting things because what's the point? I have no say about what I wear, what I play with or even very much about how I spend my time. But these things kept coming to mind, and I was really getting mad at myself for spending my time on all this wishing when in walked Daddy one Saturday afternoon, his arms all loaded up with boxes—two for each of us, and it wasn't even Christmas.

We each got a wool skirt and a sweater to match that Daddy picked out for us all by himself. And my skirt is extra special. It's plaid, and it's reversible, which means you can turn it inside-out and still wear it. Imagine that. It's like having two different skirts, or like having a secret side, one that's just as good as the side you can see. I hadn't been thinking I wanted a reversible plaid skirt and matching sweater, but since I've gotten the outfit, I don't want to wear anything else. It's full of the most beautiful colors I've ever in my life seen. The sweater is a shade of green that I could look at all day. It's like maybe if you started with one of those Fannie Mae melt-away mints, the little cubes covered in green, then added some green like from a Christmas tree, and then some royal blue, and then maybe some charcoal gray.

Daddy says the sweater brings out the green in my eyes. Just looking at it makes me wish I were a cat so I could snuggle up to it and purr. And I don't even like cats. Mommy says they're mean and all they ever do is scratch up people's furniture. My skirt has a lot of the green that's in the sweater, plus charcoal gray and a beautiful dark blue, and a little bit of warm brownish gray too. One side has more green and blue, and the other side has more green and gray. I guess making a reversible plaid works a little like the knitting and purling I learned about in Brownie Scouts. The same stitch will make one pattern on one side and a completely different pattern on the other.

When I put the outfit on it feels different than all my other clothes. It feels right. It doesn't rumple up anywhere or bunch up under my arms. It doesn't have two inches of this see-through fluffy stuff Mommy sews onto the bottoms of my dresses after there's no more hem to let down. It may be the first really nice clothing anybody's gotten me, aside from the O'Neills. I wish Daddy would buy my clothes all the time, but I wouldn't want to say that because I don't think Mommy would take to the idea.

Mommy didn't take it too well when I suggested that Kathy, Mary Ruth and I go shoe shopping with her after Miss Dixon told us that whenever we get a new pair of shoes we should have our feet measured by the salesman. This is because our feet are growing all the time and it's not good to squish your toes up with shoes that are too small.

When I told Mommy about this she said, "If Miss Dixon

is so concerned about your shoes, Laura, she can just buy them for you herself."

Since then I've been really worried because Mommy has been bringing me shoes that are too small for just about as long as I can remember. And now my little toes are starting to grow on top of the ones next to them, and all the other toes except my big toes are curling under a little bit. The pain of the shoes I can forget about. They just hurt for a little while when I put them on each morning, and then the pain goes away. But now I worry that my feet are going to be really freaky. The only thing that makes me feel better about this is that since I always have my shoes on, except when I'm in bed, nobody ever sees my feet anyway.

Another surprise, which wasn't so good, was that Mommy stopped giving me potatoes to eat for a while. She didn't say why. Just one day she passed my plate by as she was scooping out nice big spoons full of creamy mashed potatoes for everybody else. I looked up at her, and she said, "What are you looking at, Laura. You know you don't like potatoes."

How could I know that? I've always eaten all the mashed potatoes on my plate. I like potatoes mashed, fried, baked—all kinds of ways—in potato salad too. I don't get it. The only thing I can figure is that it must have something to do with her trying to keep me small. She's still giving Mary Ruth double and triple helpings. I haven't seen her do anything strange to Kathy's food. But she does say that Kathy is too skinny and that's because she eats too many vinegary things like dill pickles and little white cocktail onions.

I'd like to talk to Daddy about at least some of this. I don't like being so different from the other kids at school. I'd like to go along to the shoe store like they do, and I'd like to play with kids in my class after school, and even sometimes on Saturday. I'd limit myself to those requests if I could ask, but I've never tried talking to Daddy about anything. I'm pretty sure whatever problem I have, if it's with Mommy, he'll take her side. So I don't know when I'll ever get up the nerve to ask him.

I did get up the nerve to ask him about Kaisery though because one day he drove off in Kaisery and came back in a white Ford Galaxy. Big smile on his face.

"Where's Kaisery?" I asked.

"Junkyard where it belongs," he said.

"Junkyard? Kaisery's in a junkyard? Why?"

"The car broke down," he said

"What happened?"

"The brakes wouldn't' work anymore and couldn't be fixed. The Galaxy's better. You'll see."

That's what he thinks. He doesn't seem to remember that Kaisery's a member of our family. But I know, and I'm not going to forget. The only bad experience I ever had in Kaisery was one day when Daddy was so mad at the three of us for spitting on each other that he told us to get in the car. We piled into the back seat, and he got in the driver's seat. He started Kaisery's engine and said he was going to drive us to Mantino and drop us off there. He said he didn't want us anymore. My stomach just about fell through the floorboard at that. But then all three of us started to wail at the top of our lungs, and he turned off the engine and told us to get out of the car and behave. Now he's gone and taken Kaisery to a Mantino for cars nobody wants anymore.

So, except for getting my reversible skirt, fourth grade hasn't been such a great year. Halloween is what set the stage for me with the kids in class. I like the dressing up part, but all day long every Halloween I feel woozy in my stomach, like I'm at the edge of a high dive about to jump off. But I always get through it, and the next day the weird feeling is gone. This past year I was a ghost, an easy costume because all you have to do is cut out holes for your eyes, nose and mouth in an old sheet, slip it on over your clothes, and you're all set. When we walked into class in our costumes, Miss Dixon had us all stand up in front of class and guess who was who. As soon as somebody identified you, you sat down at your desk.

One by one all the pirates, princesses, pumpkins, and sailors got identified and joined the guessers. As each of my classmates was picked out and had to walk back to his or her seat I was gloating about how good my costume was. I thought maybe it was even the best in the class. When it got down to just three of us up there my heart was pounding real fast, kind of like when I've found a hiding place in hide-and-seek that nobody can find no matter how hard they look. Then it was just two of us, me and another ghost. And then it was just me up there. There was this long pause. A very long pause. Nobody could figure out who I was. Finally Miss Dixon said, "Well, just think of who's missing."

That didn't help. The pause continued while everybody looked around and tried to figure out who wasn't there. Finally Brad cracked a smile and said, "Oh, I know. It's just Laura."

But that's only part of how the year has gone for me. It's been like Neapolitan ice cream with its three different stripes of flavor. I only like the chocolate, but when Mommy serves it up, I have to eat all three. And now Miss Dixon says it's time to go. We're lining up at the door. We'll walk in a line downstairs to the main door, but once that door opens, we'll all burst free and fan out into the summer. I'll run away from here as fast as I can and it's like I'll be eating chocolate all the way until September.

I stood at the altar, Hank at my side, and my parents far behind when I was suddenly lifted into a cold, white cloud, floating above my wedding. I realized then that I really was saying good-bye to everything I was groomed to be. I looked up and saw Jesus floating just above me, shaking his head. Tears flowed down his cheeks as he repeated, inconsolably, "My child, my child, my child." I had broken his heart; he didn't want me to get married. Why oh why did he wait until that moment to give me a sign?

I could not return, even when we kissed as man and wife, even when the photographer's voice yanked me down to take pictures. Pictures to be put in albums for my family and for me to save, to show each other, to show our children when we got old. It's all recorded now. I am with my husband on the church stairs right after our sacramental union. He, a twinkle in his eyes, and me, a rigid face trying to conceal my shock and despair.

Mary Agnes

The Luckiest Girl

One after the other, a waterfall of wonderful things has been flowing my way. Some are as little as a ladybug landing on my sleeve for a short visit. Some are so big that they'd get me doing cartwheels all across the front lawn if I could ever get the courage to hurl my legs over me straight into the air. If I had to live this year all over again, there's not much I would change. We just got back from our longest vacation ever—two weeks in Florida, staying in the Palm Beach mansion of Mr. T.R. Stepan, owner of Stepan Chemical Company where Daddy's been working for the past few years. And now the carnival's in town for the Fourth of July. And that means rides, games, all sorts of excitement. Plus fireworks lighting up the sky on the Fourth.

One big deal is that I met Mr. Stepan in one of his mansions on a private road somewhere outside of Chicago. Kathy, Mary Ruth, Mommy and I got all dressed up. I wore an outfit from the O'Neills. This was back in October, and my outfit was full of autumn colors—a full brown skirt with a flower pattern. The blooms had tiny petals in yellow, burgundy and orange. The blouse was white with trim on the sleeves, collar and down the front panel, where the buttons are, that matched the skirt.

Mommy bought new clothes for the occasion because Daddy said the flower print, elastic waist, zipper front dresses she wears spring, summer, winter and fall aren't the kind of thing you can wear to a millionaire's house. So she had on a nice fitted gray wool skirt and white sweater. Best of all she got her hair done in soft curls by a real hairdresser, not by her friend Florence who always frizzes her hair in bunches on the ends in a style that was supposedly popular in the '40s. There's an autographed picture of Hedy Lamarr in our basement with that hairstyle. I can tell from that picture that what Florence does to Mommy's hair is a really bad imitation of the totally out of date real thing. So finally, here it is 1960, and Mommy's done something that makes her look a little bit more like the other mothers in town.

We met Mr. Stepan because Daddy was up for a big promotion. That was an exciting thing—Daddy being in line for something really big. It was down to him and this man he works with named Ron Landis. For months this whole seeing who's the right man for the job went on and on. We had to have people from Daddy's work over to our house for Sunday dinner. Sometimes they brought their wives and children. And sometimes we had to go to their houses too. We had some of Daddy's co-workers over so often, they were starting to feel a little bit like family.

Part of Mr. Stepan's decision was based on how well Daddy and Ron Landis trained people to do their jobs. I remember Daddy spending an entire weekend in his and Mommy's room with poster board and tempera paint drawing pictures of chemicals flowing through pipes with arrows showing the direction things were moving, and colors changing when different chemicals combined. I thought they were beautiful. But later I heard Mommy complain on the phone that some of the young men being trained thought the charts were really stupid. They laughed about how seriously Daddy took his assignment, something Daddy's not used to having people do to him. It really bugged him. I think those guys must be out of their minds.

Mommy, Kathy, Mary Ruth and I did our best to be presentable when we met Mr. Stepan. I don't think there was much we could have done different. But as soon as I met Ron Landis' Breck-commercial-blonde wife and clean well-dressed children in their every-pillow-and-chair-matching, two-story house with, of course, sod and perfect landscaping, I suspected we couldn't hold a candle to them. I tried my best to hope somehow we could. It's a similar feeling I get when I go to any of the O'Neill houses, especially Uncle Jim's. He's a doctor just like Grampa O'Neill. Every piece of furniture seems exactly right, and the carpet and drapes—it all comes together like a home in a magazine, a home you can't imagine someone really living in.

Our house is just a hodgepodge of odd things stuck here and there. And that's how the three of us look too, even if we're wearing dresses from the O'Neills. There are still our slips, which are falling apart, pinned up, and not necessarily the right style for what we're wearing. Our shoes are usually wearing out in places that we hope nobody will notice. And our hair is, well, dirty and never cut in an actual style. It's hard to feel like we can stand shoulder to shoulder with our cousins or with Ron Landis' family and not feel somehow like we're just oozing some sort of rancid grease.

While this evaluation of Daddy and Ron Landis was going on, I was sure that all of that wouldn't matter too much because Daddy is so brilliant. Not too long ago there was this disagreement about a formula for some new sort of soap. Daddy was the only one who disagreed with the formula people were planning to use. He said, "If you do that, it'll all turn into jelly." But the others disagreed and went ahead with their plan. That night Daddy got a phone call. After he hung up he jumped up in the air, clicked his heels together, and danced all around the dining room and living room because now his co-workers were faced with two enormous vats of jelly to dispose of. I just had to get up and dance with him too. Daddy's more right about stuff like that than anybody. I thought Daddy was sure to get the big promotion.

But in the end the big job went to Ron Landis. I heard Mommy and Daddy saying something about him having a better degree than Daddy has. Daddy went to teacher's college because he wanted to be a science teacher. At the time he went to school, it was only a two-year thing, learning to be a teacher. For some reason though when Daddy was looking for teaching jobs the only ones he was offered in Chicago were jobs teaching P.E., and he didn't want to teach P.E. Then he was away in Panama during World War II. I think he worked on chemicals there. When he got back home he gave up on teaching and started working as a chemical engineer for Darling & Company. Then he switched to Stepan because he said it offered better opportunities.

Not getting the big promotion was a disappointment for Daddy, but he got a different sort of promotion with a big raise as, I guess, a sort of compensation prize to ease the pain of losing out on the big cheese thing. Now he's one of the executives of the company. The executives get to take vacations at Mr. Stepan's Palm Beach mansion when Mr. Stepan doesn't want to use it. That leaves most of the summer at the mansion free because it's too hot and humid for Mr. Stepan. So we left for the mansion right after school got out for the summer.

Daddy first told us about going to Florida one Saturday after lunch in our dining room. He was so happy that he took one of the charcoal pencils from a drawing kit Kathy had nearby, and he drew a palm tree right on the wall.

"May we draw too?" Kathy asked.

"Sure," he said, "Let's draw what we think Florida will look like."

I ran to the box of treasures I keep under my bed and found a postcard of a pelican with fish at its feet. I started copying that, only larger than post card size. Kathy started sketching flamingoes. Mary Ruth began drawing little birds flying in the sky. Then Mommy walked in and gasped. "Hank, whatever are you doing?"

"We're drawing on the walls, dear. What does it look like we're doing? Come join us. We're drawing Florida." He began drawing mountains in the background behind the flamingoes.

She paused, studying the wall and then said, "Do you really think there are mountains in Florida?"

"Oh, what does it matter? This is our idea of Florida," Daddy replied.

Mommy left the room and came back with a load of little jars of oil paints leftover from our various paint-by-number kits done over the years. She also had some tubes of real oil paint that Daddy gave her back when we lived on Richmond Street.

"I think it needs some color, don't you?" she said, holding out the paints to us.

"Yes, yes!" we all agreed.

All afternoon we worked on the mural of Florida. It has a bright blue sky with fluffy white clouds and birds flying overhead. The mountains are different shades of orange, red, rust, white and brown where Daddy and Mary Ruth painted furiously. Sometimes we painted over each other's work, laughing so hard. Mommy said we sounded like a pack of wild hyenas. The mural has three palm trees that Daddy sketched and we all helped paint, and my pelican with fish at his webbed feet, looking like they've been dead a little too long to eat. Kathy's flamingoes hunt for fish in a deep blue lake. There's a giant succulent that Mommy copied from a magazine photo, and there are little tufts of grass all over in the sand. Boy, were we proud when we finished. We're the only family I know that's ever painted their own mural on their dining room wall.

Another thing Daddy's promotion means is that he might get sent to Italy to be in charge of some company dealings there. If that happens, we may all be off to Italy within months. I think that would be so exciting, to live in a whole different country with a completely different language for a while. Plus I'd get to see the Leaning Tower of Pizza, one of the seven wonders of the world, I think. Plus, Daddy says even if we don't go to Italy, we're going to move from Hinsdale. For quite a while now he's had a long commute. He has to drive all the way to a place called Northfield. Sometimes, if he puts in an extra long day, he even sleeps on a cot in his office. He says we'll be moving either to Northfield or a place near it to make things easier on him. That is, if we don't move to Italy for a year or two first.

We already went looking at houses in a subdivision near there. They had three different models: a ranch house, a bilevel house and a regular sort of two-story house. I like the two-story one the best. Kathy, Mary Ruth and I waltzed around the empty rooms. There were enough of them for each of us to have our own room. We even decided whose would be whose. I was standing in the one I wanted for my own, looking out the window to the thick green lawn and the little elm trees near the curb. Daddy walked in and said, "You really like this house, don't you?"

And I said, "Oh, yes, Daddy, yes! Can we buy it?"

And he said, "We'll see. You know, your mother likes the ranch house."

I must have looked real disappointed at this because he said, "Cheer up. We haven't decided anything. We're just looking, for now. We may be going to Italy for a while, after all."

I figure either way it would be great. Italy or near Daddy's office would both be a thrill, even though I had a great year in school this past year, my last year at Madison School. I got really lucky and got Mrs. Daniels for my teacher. She's the best and nicest teacher in the entire school. She's pretty too with big round brown eyes, and dark wavy hair down to her shoulders. She's real slim too and wears these crisp clean outfits. She looks kind of like a model, only not so skinny.

I'm sure everybody in class loved her just like I did. And the great thing is that she loved all of us too. It's such a snug feeling to be in a group where you feel like everybody belongs. I don't know exactly how it happens. I don't know what Mrs. Daniels did to make her classroom such a special place to be, but it was easy to be there every minute of every school day. Right from the start I began to notice that on Sunday afternoons I'd catch myself actually looking forward to Monday when I could go to school and see Mrs. Daniels. That was a brand new feeling and totally shocked me. If I could know that every year in Hinsdale would be like the year I just finished, I'd want to stay, but from what Kathy says about junior high school, I'm dreading even setting one foot in the door—I have been for the past two years since Kathy started sixth grade.

Kathy drew me a little chart of how things are socially. There's the center like a bull's-eye where the really popular kids are. She says not too many kids from Madison School have a chance of getting in there. It's mostly kids from other schools in richer parts of town. Then there's the first circle around the bull's-eye. Those are the kids who sometimes hang out with the popular kids and are considered okay by them. And the circles go out like that, ring after ring growing less and less popular. Kathy says she's in the absolute outermost ring, the most unpopular, and that's where I'll probably be too, especially since this past year I wore my reversible skirt to school three days a week when the weather wasn't too warm for it. On Mondays I wore the blue/green side with the matching sweater. On Wednesdays I wore the gray/green side with the same sweater. Then on Fridays I wore the blue/green side again with a long sleeved white blouse. I felt so good in Mrs. Daniels's class I don't even know if anybody noticed. But Kathy says in junior high, if I wear the skirt more than once a week, no matter which side is showing, nobody will even talk to me.

How could I look forward to something like that? I thought maybe having kids mix together from different grammar schools would make it easier for everybody to fit in, like there'd be more room. I keep hoping that things will be different for me. I feel partly responsible for Kathy's bad luck because we were playing blind man about a week before she started sixth grade. When we play that we always lead each other into things even though we promise each other that we won't. It was Kathy's turn to be led, and I promised I wouldn't lead her into anything, planning to do just the opposite, as usual. I must have been really convincing because she believed me. But I didn't know she believed me. I led her smack into one of our clothes poles.

Blood came streaming down her face because the lenses of her glasses broke and cut into her skin. At first it looked like the blood was spurting right out of her eye. Mary Ruth screamed so loud at the sight of blood flowing down Kathy's face and onto her blouse that Mommy came outside and started yelling. It took a while for all of us to settle down and take a closer look and see that the blood was coming from a gash just above her eyebrow. There's just a little scar there now, but Kathy had to start sixth grade with a big gauze patch taped above her eye. Plus she had her giant glasses on too. So that didn't help with the first impression people got of her. I do feel pretty bad about that, but I think she's forgiven me by now. Things are so much nicer all the way around at home now than they were back when Kathy started sixth grade.

The biggest thing that happened, and I mean a super super huge thing, this past year happened during the first month of school. Grampa Adams fell down in his room and broke his hip. Kathy, Mary Ruth and I weren't home when it happened. We missed the ambulance and all the excitement. Mommy said she wasn't too worried though because it was a common thing for older people to break hips like that because their bones are weaker. She said it wasn't life threatening, like a massive heart attack or something. She went to visit him every day, and gave us little reports on how he was doing. He seemed to be fine. But then one day she came home and said he'd caught pneumonia in the hospital, and he was very sick. The very next day when I was home from school for lunch the phone rang and Mommy picked it up. I watched her nod her head real slow saying, "Yes. Yes. I understand. Thank you. I will. Okay. Yes. Good-bye."

Then she hung the phone up real fast and gasped, like maybe somebody had just poked something real sharp into her back. She put her head down and leaned both her hands on the counter as though she were about to fall down. She looked up at me, and her eyes were full of tears. In all the years I've known Mommy, that's the only time I've seen that. Then she said, "My father's dead. Grampa Adams is dead." And a couple of tears rolled down her face. I ran over to her and hugged her real hard. I almost cried myself. Mommy was so upset it made me feel real sad for her.

Pretty soon it was time for me to go back to school. I headed out the door. I was walking along, head down, just feeling like I was swimming through Mommy's sadness. I saw Jillie's friend Diane walking toward me. She said, "Laura, you look different. What's wrong with you?"

"Grampa Adams died," I said on the verge of tears.

"What are you crying about? All he ever was, was mean to you," she snapped. Then she ran off to catch up with some other kids walking to the school playground.

This startled me because Diane and I aren't friends. I've never talked with her about my family, and she's never said a word to me about hers. I didn't know how she could know the first thing about how Grampa Adams treated me. It also startled me because I thought maybe she was right. Maybe I had no reason to be sad. He was really mean to me. That was the truth, but then I thought about how sad Mommy was and I was really confused.

For the rest of that day and then in the following days at Grampa Adams' wake and funeral I thought about my feelings. I realized how very little feeling I had for him, and what a relief it was to me that he was gone. He had poked his bony fingers in my face and lectured me about my badness for the very last time. Mary Ruth and I went up to his coffin and stared at his purply face full of pancake makeup. We dared each other to touch him. We each reached in and touched his hand. It was cold and hard. Daddy noticed that we were hovering there and he came over to us and said, "Move away from there now girls; people will think you're morbid."

Once Grampa Adams was buried, none of us talked about what was going on, but it seemed to me that deep inside each and every one of us was celebrating—even Mommy. It was like there'd been a big steel band around the house and all the drapes were drawn making it a tight and dark place. Then Grampa Adams' death broke the band and lifted the drapes. Everywhere there was sunshine and bursts of laughter from Kathy, Mary Ruth and me, and a whole lot more hugs and affectionate little kisses between Mommy and Daddy. We seem like a brand new family now.

One of the first things Daddy did after Grampa Adams' funeral was scoop up old Rusty. The dog growled and snapped, but he had stopped eating and was just lying all day on the floor by the piano. Every so often he tried to get up, and his legs would slide right out from under him. So Daddy took him off to the Hinsdale Animal Shelter and had him filled with poison so he'd die. They call it putting an animal to sleep. I gave Daddy a squinty-eyed look because I could tell he was happy to be getting rid of Rusty. I wasn't sure if it was right, him being so happy. I was thinking maybe we should try taking him to a vet first even though he was the meanest dog I'd ever met. He was the only dog we had. Daddy looked at me scowling at him as he walked toward the door and said, "He can't live without Grampa Adams, Laura. He's heartbroken. He can hardly walk, and he's going blind. We have to put him out of his misery."

I was sure all of this was true. I guess I was just feeling guilty about all of this happiness resulting from Grampa Adams' death. Mommy cleared out Grampa Adams' room, packing most of his things up into cardboard boxes and driving them off to Good Will. Her cousin Muriel's oldest boy, Mark, came and picked up the old Nash and drove it away.

Big teenaged boys like him love to take old cars like that and turn them into hot rods.

Then Mommy and Daddy moved Kathy's bed and dresser into Grampa Adams' old room. Kathy, being the oldest, there was never any question about anybody other than her moving into the room. But that meant Mary Ruth and I got to spread out a little bit in our room too. That was nice, like being able to take in a great big gulp of air after having a contest with someone over how long you can hold your breath. Since I'd finally gotten a real twin-sized bed in fourth grade, we'd been really cramped. Now our beds are far enough apart so that Mary Ruth wouldn't roll over and sock me in the mouth in her sleep by mistake.

Kathy's having her own room means we don't fight quite as much because we're not bumping into each other all the time. Plus, now we have a new place to gather. When Kathy says it's okay for Mary Ruth and me to visit her room, it calls for a new way of acting. That's not something we decided, it's just something that happened. When we gather in Kathy's room we actually talk a little bit about what we think, something we've never done before. The first time we had a little meeting was one morning when Mommy was having a bad spell, and she was really running Kathy down. Overall, she's been much calmer and nicer since Grampa Adams' death, but every so often, something snaps, and her ugly side comes out like a great big fart in a small, crowded room.

Kathy was in the kitchen washing some dishes and Mommy started going on about her high falutin' ways. She said, "You probably think you're too good to be doing these dishes, don't you. Think you'd rather be somewhere else. I know you."

"I'm just doing the—"

"Wipe that look off your face, Missy. Your attitude, your attitude stinks."

"I'm just trying to get the dishes done like you asked, okay?"

"No, it's not okay. Who do you think you are?" Mommy's voice was loud and fast. She started repeating herself and moving closer to Kathy until she was right beside her, practically screaming into her ear. Kathy threw the dishrag into the sink, ran out of the kitchen into her room and closed the door. I hated to see this, but I was also relieved that this time it wasn't my turn to get Mommy's tongue lashing.

Mary Ruth and I swooped over to her door and started hovering, not knowing what to do. Mommy looked over from the kitchen and said, "Get away from there you two. Leave her royal highness alone."

We backed away a little bit, but as soon as she had her back turned we opened the door just a couple of inches and Mary Ruth asked, "Can we come in?"

"Go ahead. I don't care," Kathy said. So we slipped in and closed the door behind us. Kathy was on her bed, and Mary Ruth and I sat cross-legged on the floor near her.

"Mommy's gonna be real mad if she catches us in here," I said.

"She's not our mother," Kathy said.

"I know that," said Mary Ruth.

"Me too," I said.

There was a long pause as we looked at each other. None of us had ever said that to each other before. It felt like saying this might be wrong, but it also felt really good, like we were breaking a rule, and nobody knew it but us.

"Our mother was Mary Agnes," I said.

"That's right," said Mary Ruth.

"And she killed herself," Kathy said.

"Yeah, she hung herself with a rope." Mary Ruth added.

There was another long pause as the three of us thought about this together for the first time.

"Do either of you remember her?" I asked.

"Not really," said Kathy.

"Me neither," said Mary Ruth, "except I remember something about walking home from a party, and there was nobody home. It was getting dark outside and cold."

"Yes, me too," Kathy said. "I think it was Halloween. We were at the neighbor's house, and we bobbed for apples."

A chill ran up my spine. "I used to dream all the time about coming home all dressed up in party clothes and nobody was home. I haven't dreamt it lately, but I used to have it almost every night."

"How does the dream go?" Kathy asked.

So I described my dream where I stand on a path leading to a door and the two of them are way ahead of me. First Kathy tries to open the front door, but it won't open. She says, "There's nobody home," and she races off to the back of the house. Then Mary Ruth does the same thing, and I'm left there alone on the path, frightened, unable to move, and not knowing what to do.

"Wow, Laur, you dream that? I remember that and being inside, on the basement stairs," Kathy said. "Our mother was dangling with a rope around her neck, and I was trying to get her to talk to me."

Then a scene flashed into my mind. I saw myself going down some stairs to a basement and walking under long legs dangling in the air. Then I was climbing back up the stairs. Kathy and Mary Ruth were standing close together, frowning, and saying they needed to get our mother down. I didn't think it was our mother hanging there because whatever or whoever it was down in the basement wasn't acting at all like our mother. Just when I got to the top of the stairs Mary Ruth said she was going to look for scissors.

My thoughts were interrupted by Mary Ruth's voice. "I think I went to look for scissors to cut her down," she said.

"And I remember sitting on the stairs next to her, trying to undo the knot," Kathy said.

"I was just seeing that happening," I said. "I think I followed Mary Ruth. I didn't go to look for scissors. I went to look for Mommy because I thought maybe she wasn't really hanging in the basement. I thought maybe she was playing hide-and-seek. I think I followed Mary Ruth from room to room and upstairs to the bedrooms. She was opening drawers, looking for scissors, and I was looking under the beds and in the closets to see if Mommy was hiding inside." I said.

"I remember that. And I headed back to tell Kathy I couldn't find the scissors, but Daddy was there in the kitchen at the top of the basement stairs. He told me to stop, to stay away," Mary Ruth said. "He was furious. He had Kathy by the arm. He must have pulled her up the stairs."

"Oh, gosh. This is creepy," I said. "Right now I think I'm remembering running as fast as I can behind you, and Daddy says, 'Stop, don't go downstairs,' but I am running so fast I can't stop. He's reaching down and grabbing us both with his free hand, the one not holding Kathy. He was scary mad."

"Yeah. I think that's right," Mary Ruth said, "but I don't remember what happened after that."

"I don't remember either, except for staying at our neighbor's that night," Kathy said.

"Really? You remember that?" I asked. "I've always had this weird memory that just seems to come out of nowhere of some lady sticking me in a car and speeding away so fast. I'm on the floor in the front seat bouncing around with one hand on the glove compartment and one hand on the seat trying to keep steady. Everything inside me is vibrating with the car, and the lady's looking at me real strange, like she's seen a ghost, but I don't know why. I don't know who she was or where she took me. But I think maybe it was before you two went to Mantino though."

"I wonder how long we were there," Mary Ruth said.

"I remember visiting you there," I said.

"You're kidding, right?" Kathy asked. "I just remember crying into my pillow at night, and the nuns kept telling me to stop, but I couldn't."

Just then Mommy opened the door to Kathy's room and said, "Ah you two, I told you not to go in here. Get out and get busy. Leave her royal highness alone."

Mary Ruth and I got up to get to work. At the side of the house, there was a gigantic pile of smelly black manure that was just delivered. Mommy loved to order manure. One of our jobs was to shovel it into the back garden area and lawn before it got too far into the cold weather that things started to freeze up. Mary Ruth and I didn't talk about our conversation while we worked that day. We haven't talked about it since then either, or mentioned our mother's suicide at all. But just knowing that my dream is more than a dream, knowing it's a little chunk of a memory, that sets something in me at ease a little bit. I still don't feel anything like love for the mommy who brought me into this world. I just feel this awful emptiness, so cold, even worse than having to stay outside in the winter wind because this cold is coming from the inside.

Every now and then when some grown-up meets the three of us they'll say, "My goodness, three in a row? Only a year apart. That must have been hard on your mother." And I think, well, maybe if I'd never been born it wouldn't have been so hard and she'd be alive. I feel like an expression Mommy says sometimes—the straw that broke the camel's back. It was me, me, me! It wasn't Kathy and Mary Ruth's being bad. It was me coming along to the wrong family at the wrong time. I think the O'Neills must be really mad at me for ending her life by starting mine. My life took her from them, but they own her and they're guarding her like a treasure. Daddy seems to think she never existed at all. But I know now that she did exist, and that I saw her hanging dead in the basement. It makes me wonder what's going on inside of Daddy's head. Not that I'd ever ask.

Another thing that happened this year is that I had a boyfriend for two days. His name is Jake. Mommy saw me looking at our class picture, and she asked me, "Do you like anybody?"

And I felt really shy about saying anything, but I pointed to this guy Jake and said, "I like him."

"Does he like you?"

"I don't know. He asked to play with my wooden ball puzzle the other day, and he thanked me when he returned it."

Mommy rummaged through one of her junk drawers and pulled out a little wooden puzzle in the shape of a boat, and asked, "Do you want to give this to him?"

I thought that was a fine idea and I said, "Oh, could I?"

So she found a ribbon to put around it, and the next day during recess I gave it to him. "Thanks," he said, "Do you want to go to the youth center tomorrow?"

"I can't go tomorrow, but I might be able to go on Friday next week," I said, having to stick with Mommy's rule about no playing with anybody after school except on Fridays and having to ask a whole week in advance.

Mommy said it would be okay, and finally Friday rolled around. Jake and I walked side by side to the youth center. Once inside we sat on a couple of chairs, just swinging our feet, nothing much to say. Finally he asked, "So, do you want some gum?"

"Yep," I said.

So we headed to the vending machine. He put a couple of nickels in the slot, pushed the button for cinnamon gum, the only kind they had. We listened to the machine rattle and then watched the gum fall down and land in the bin. He picked it up and handed it to me.

"Thanks," I said, rolling it around in my palm.

"Welcome," he replied.

Then we went back to the chairs and sat for a little while. Finally I said, "I guess I'd better be goin'."

"Me too," he said. We left the youth center, walking together a couple of blocks; then he turned left and I turned right, and that was the end of my having a boyfriend because we haven't talked since.

There is something I would change about fifth grade if I could. When our vision was tested, I got to take home a note that said I needed to see an eye doctor. At last, I was in the car, with Uncle Dean driving, Grampa in the passenger seat in front, and Kathy, Mary Ruth and me lined up in the back. We were heading for Dr. Sullivan's office. After all these years of just the two of them going off with Grampa to see Dr. Sullivan, I was going too.

We sat in a waiting room surrounded on three sides with cases full of all different sorts of glasses. All different colors and shapes. First Dr. Sullivan called Kathy in, then Mary Ruth, and then me. He put drops in my eyes to make the pupils really big. Then after a little wait he sat me in a big leather chair in a very dark room and held up this telescope sort of thing and told me to look at a chart full of letters that were in a circle of light on the wall. He changed the lenses, click, click, click in his machine until I could see the bottom line perfectly. Then he wrote some numbers down on a form and handed it to Grampa O'Neill.

I didn't get any of the glasses at Dr. Sullivan's office because Mommy says his glasses are too expensive. She says the places where they sell glasses in Hinsdale are even more expensive. A couple of days after seeing Dr. Sullivan, Mommy drove us to some discount place on a busy, wide street in a suburb close to the city, and Mommy picked out my glasses for me. They were the cheapest ones in the cheapest row, some kind of strange blue metallic sparkly things. It took a couple of days for them to be ready, but soon we drove back to pick them up, and the man in charge of sales put them on me to make sure the ear pieces were nice and snug on my head.

After a couple of days of wearing the things I decided I'd had enough. I left them on my dresser and came out to breakfast. Mommy noticed right away and said, "Where are your glasses, Laura?"

"On my dresser," I said, reaching for a knife to slice a piece of chocolate ranch cake.

Mommy said, "You're supposed to wear them all the time, like your shoes. You only take them off when you go to bed."

"I don't need them all the time. I see everything fine right now."

"We didn't go to all that expense so you could just keep a pair of glasses on your dresser. Now go put them on."

So I had to go back and put them on. I've been wearing them all the time since then. Nobody knows how hard I tried to become nearsighted, how I used to practice not looking far, pretending everything was blurry—just so I could see what it was like to go with Grampa O'Neill to Dr. Sullivan's office. I wish I never had gone to all that trouble. But who knows, even if I hadn't practiced being nearsighted, I might have still needed glasses anyway. There's no way of telling. And I'm stuck with these really stupid-looking glasses forever. I hate them, absolutely hate them, especially since Kathy says just wearing glasses in junior high school is like having ten strikes against you right off the bat before you've even said a word. Now when I look in the mirror, the glasses are the first thing I see about me, and I get mad at myself for ever being foolish enough to want them.

I even had to wear my glasses to the beach in Florida. Mr. Stepan and his neighbors have a private beach—only people living or invited to stay in the houses right nearby can go to the beach at the end of the road. Nobody from Miami, West Palm Beach, or even other parts of Palm Beach can just drive up, pile out of the car, spread their beach towels out on the sand, and settle in. They'd get booted out. That makes the place pretty empty. When we went to the beach we were the only ones there, except for the pelicans and these wonderful lizards called chameleons. They dart really fast across the road into the sand, and they change color depending on what they're sitting on. None of us had ever been on a private beach before. It was quite a privilege.

Mr. Stepan's home isn't just an empty place to stay. There's a maid there and a gardener too. The maid always had some breakfast for us. One of the things she makes is fruit salad, and one of the fruits is mango. She cuts it into half-inch chunks. It is so good—juicy, sweet as well as tart, and sort of nutty tasting. The maid was always cleaning up after us too. The gardener cut fresh orchids from Mr. Stepan's garden for us each morning and put them in a vase on the dining room table. I loved the orchids. I've decided they're my favorite flower. I asked Mommy if we could grow them at home, and she said, "No, they're a tropical flower. They'll only grow in a hot, humid climate."

"Can we buy some at a flower shop every now and then?"

"You can just wipe that thought out of your mind, Missy. They're much too expensive." And that was the end of that.

It sure was blazing hot there. It gets hot in Hinsdale in the summer, but not like that. It was so scorching that if we stayed out in the sun too long sweat just started pouring out of our skin in places we've never sweated from before. And we'd get little beads of sweat on our skin where the nosepieces and earpieces of our glasses touch. Sometimes Mommy said she thought she was going to faint from the heat. That didn't surprise me because she's the sickly one in our family. She limps, she's deaf in one ear, she scratches her elbows raw and she's always reaching one of her arms behind her back so she can rub a fist up and down her miserable spine. She's not strong and healthy like Kathy, Mary Ruth, Daddy and me.

The bedroom that Mary Ruth and I shared had white carpets. Kathy had a room of her own, which was nice for her, but she missed out on being surrounded by white. It was like being in a land of snow, only it wasn't cold. It was the room of one of Mr. Stepan's children. When Mommy first saw the white rug she said, "Imagine that, white carpet in a child's room. I guess if you're a millionaire you can afford to replace the rug if your kids wreck it."

Daddy and Mommy said Mary Ruth and I had to be real careful not to track dirt into that room. We always checked our feet before we went in there, plus our hands and all the rest of us too because the bedspreads are white too. We didn't want to leave prints and spots on those any more than we wanted to track dirt in on the floor.

The maid made our beds each morning. Mommy told us the first morning that we should make our beds, but Daddy disagreed. He said, "Oh, Helen, the maid will just remake them anyway. Let the girls enjoy getting waited on."

I was watching real close to see what she would do, half hoping there'd be a fight. Only once in my life have I ever seen them fight. I only really caught the end of that, where Mommy and Grampa Adams stormed out the door, got into the old Nash, and drove off in a huff. We burn papers in this huge can in the corner of our backyard. The fight had something to do with how you should stack the papers in the can, where you should put the newspapers in relation to everything else, like the used tissues and crinkled up envelopes and such. Mommy and Grampa Adams were gone a long time fuming about the paper burning.

That afternoon, Daddy was downstairs in this little office section of the basement near the washer and dryer. It was unusual for him not to be in his workshop area. He was looking at a photo album I'd never seen before. I was still small enough to ride a trike back then, barely. I rode it around in circles near him, keeping him company. If I could have told him I would have said, "Everything will be okay, Daddy. We don't need them." But I didn't say anything like that. I just kept riding in circles.

At the end of the day Mommy and Grampa Adams came back. That was all there was to their big fight. That was so long ago, I figured it was time for another one, especially since they were disagreeing about something so big as whether Kathy, Mary Ruth, and I should make our own beds in Mr. Stepan's mansion. But Mommy didn't get worked up. She just said, "Oh, I guess you're right, Hank. I just don't want them to think they can get away with it at home. I'm not a maid service, you know."

"When I make my first million, dear, you'll have your own maid service," he said, leaning over to give her a big kiss square on the lips.

I knew he meant it. Daddy talks like that from time to time, saying that someday he'll be a millionaire. I have no doubt that he will be. Somebody as smart and wonderful as he is just has to succeed. He also says Kathy's going to be a great artist, and Mary Ruth has the makings of a great scientist. He says I'm going to grow up and be Miss America and marry my own millionaire. That's fun to think about, but really, I don't think most people think I'm pretty enough for that, especially with these glasses I have to wear all the time now.

And then there's my wardrobe too. I don't think any Miss America would be caught dead in some the getups I wear. Daddy thinks it was our shabby clothes at the tollbooth near Palm Beach that caused him to be insulted. He pulled the Galaxy up to the booth, handed the toll taker some change, and asked him for directions to Palm Beach. The man peered long into the car, front and back seats and said, "Are you sure you don't mean West Palm Beach?"

"No, I mean Palm Beach, sir," Daddy said.

"Because there's a difference between Palm Beach and—"

"It's Palm Beach we're going to. Which way is it?" I could see from the back seat that Daddy's ears were turning red, and that's not a good sign.

"Well, all right then, if you're sure Palm Beach is the right place—"

"Never mind. My daughters will find it faster than you can tell me." With that, Daddy put his foot on the gas pedal and we sped away. Kathy and Mary Ruth had taken turns all the way from Illinois looking at road maps and being Daddy's navigators, telling him when to turn. Every now and then one of them would get stumped, and they'd lean in real close together studying the map. As far as I was concerned the map might as well have been written in Chinese characters. It made no sense to me how it connected to the roads we were speeding along on. But my sisters did the job. Here we were almost to our destination. I was feeling sort of in awe of them and proud too because Daddy had just sort of praised them to the toll taker, but as we sped off, Daddy said, "Look at the three of you back there looking like slobs in your mismatched, filthy clothes. No wonder he thinks we belong in West Palm Beach."

I could tell from all this that Daddy thought there was something wrong with belonging in West Palm Beach, that it wasn't as good a place as Palm Beach, and it was a bad thing that somebody thought we didn't belong where we were headed. But I thought that if anybody was to blame for that it was Mommy, not me. She's the one who picks out the clothes we have on. I also wondered, how did Daddy know it was Kathy, Mary Ruth and me that made the guy think we weren't Palm Beach quality people? Maybe it was the car. Maybe it was Daddy. Maybe Mommy. I kept my mouth shut though because I figured if I said anything like that he would get so angry he just might turn the car around and drive all the way home nonstop. It wasn't worth risking our big Florida vacation over.

The first thing we did though, after we unloaded our suitcases at the mansion was go looking for a place to buy some new clothes. Of course, all the places in Palm Beach itself were too expensive. "They're ten times worse than Hinsdale stores," Mommy said, "It's not even worth going inside." We wound up in a discount store in West Palm Beach where Kathy, Mary Ruth and I got to pick out two matching sets of shorts and tops each. That was so when we were going about sightseeing at least we'd match. I could hardly believe

Mommy was letting us pick out our own clothes, but I tried to act casual, like it was no big deal, because if Mommy saw me all excited, maybe she'd change her mind. At the cash register the checkout lady pointed to some dresses on sale, but I knew Mommy wouldn't go for that. We didn't need anything new for going out to dinner. We each had brought a couple of our O'Neill outfits for that. So in a way the insult from the toll man led to me getting a couple of brand new matching shorts sets, something I've never had before. I'll get to wear them all summer long and remember this trip each time I slide them over my tanned, tanned skin.

When we go out to eat, Mommy and Daddy always decide what we eat, and Mommy always makes sure that it's the cheapest thing on the menu. Daddy gets whatever he wants. It's a farce, the three of us even looking at the menu, except I guess it's good reading practice and interesting to see what different restaurants serve. But for this entire Florida trip we got to choose our own desserts. I always picked a scoop of chocolate ice cream. Mommy got exasperated with this. She wanted me to at least try pecan pie while I was in the South. I was determined to sample the chocolate ice cream in every state between Florida and Illinois. It was all good. How could chocolate ice cream not be good? Some scoops melt faster than others, some are darker and maybe not as sweet as others, but I was in heaven with each lick. Mommy tried to get Daddy to help convince me that I shouldn't always have chocolate. She said, "It's not right, Hank. Laura's being so stubborn about her chocolate ice cream."

He replied, "We told the girls they could pick their desserts. If Laura wants to eat chocolate ice cream, if she's foolish enough to pass up pecan pie, key lime pie, and peach cobbler, and all the other great desserts that have been offered on the menus, let her do it."

"It's not right for a girl to be so obstinate. She has a stubborn streak a mile wide."

"You've got that right, dear, probably three miles wide, but I'm not going back on my word." And that was the end of that.

Choosing my dessert is not the only thing I'm going to miss about our grand Florida trip. The whole thing was out of this world, really. We passed by so many kinds of homes and people along the highways, the Smokey Mountains rising up into the sky like some sort of fairy tale kingdom, the red earth in Georgia and Alabama. We rode in a glass-bottomed boat seeing all sorts of bright-colored fish below us. We ate out every day. Somebody made our beds each morning. It was all wonderful. But the thing I loved most was having Daddy around. It was the longest time we'd ever spent together— Kathy, Mary Ruth, Mommy, Daddy, and me—and I like us. I like the way we were riding in the car, enjoying seeing new things together. I wish it could have lasted longer than two weeks. But we packed up and said good-bye to Mr. Stepan's mansion one morning. Then it was just three days together in the car, and then two days of Daddy being at home before he went back to work.

Now it's rush, rush, rush for him before he heads to work, and he's tired and busy reading the paper every night. It's not the same as eating breakfast with him every day, being on the beach with him, watching him play checkers with Kathy in Mr. Stepan's sunroom. She's getting so good he had to really concentrate to beat her. The sunroom has a wall of windows looking out onto the garden. Having all of us sitting in there after a day of swimming on the beach, reading books, newspapers, comics—it was a very happy time. The only thing that made the thought of going home more okay with me, and I think for Kathy and Mary Ruth too, is that Muffin, our little beagle was waiting in a kennel for us to pick him up. I bet he missed us something fierce.

Muffin is another one of the great things that happened in the past year. It couldn't have been more than two weeks after Daddy took Rusty to the Hinsdale Animal Shelter when late one Saturday morning, after we'd done all our usual chores, he said to Kathy, Mary Ruth and me, "Get in the car, girls. We have an errand to run."

Mommy was in the kitchen smiling, wiping her hands on a towel. I was a little suspicious, but Daddy wasn't angry. I figured it wasn't likely that he was planning to take us to Mantino or anything like that. We drove quite a long way to where there is even more space between houses than in Hinsdale. We pulled into a driveway. There was a house on one side, a garage toward the back, and on the other side a low little building with several long, narrow fenced-in areas. In those enclosures were dogs, lots of them, beagles one and all.

"This is a kennel, girls, and we've come to pick up our puppy."

A man came out, shook Daddy's hand and led us to the other side of the low building to a little pen with about half a dozen puppies. He said he'd already picked one out for us, a male, which is what Mommy and Daddy had already decided on. The man lifted the puppy up and put him in Kathy's arms. Mary Ruth and I crowded around him, and right there the three of us fell in love. He is brown with a black saddle and black on his tail and ears, and he has a white tip on his tail, white paws, a little white patch on his chest and a tiny white diamond in the center of his forehead. Some of the puppies had a lot more white on them, but I just loved that his white marks were so clean and cute.

Daddy paid the man $40—two twenty dollar bills. Kathy carried the puppy to the car. Daddy got a towel from the trunk, took the puppy from Kathy, told the three of us to get in. Then he laid the white towel across Kathy's lap and put the puppy down. Mary Ruth and I leaned in close to pat his little head. Our very own puppy. I never would have dreamed of asking for one, and now here he was sitting in Kathy's lap. We started thinking up names then and there. I don't know who thought up Muffin, but it stuck. Later on Mommy added Irish Zookie in front of Muffin on his papers for the American Kennel Club. His certificate came back Irish Zookie Muffin, XXIII. I couldn't believe anybody else was crazy enough to give a dog that name.

We went out to dinner to celebrate the night we picked Muffin up. We went to a place called the Cypress near the entrance to the Illinois Tollway. When we're not on vacation, we don't go out to eat much, so this was a big deal. Mommy ordered duck for me. I hated it so much I could only eat a couple of bites. Thank goodness we don't have to eat everything on our plates in a restaurant. There isn't time for everybody to sit around waiting in that situation.

We locked Muffin in the bathroom before we left for dinner. When we got back and opened the door, there was puppy poop all over the bathroom floor, lower cabinet doors, on the walls. It was all over Muffin too. Daddy handed Muffin to me and told me to clean him up downstairs in the utility sink and then play with him. He told Kathy and Mary Ruth to clean up the bathroom. Kathy and Mary Ruth were angry that I got to tend to Muffin and didn't have to clean up his mess. But it didn't last. We pretty much share everything to do with Muffin equally, starting right from our first efforts to house train him.

We tried to keep an eye on him and catch him before he soiled the house. Maybe about half the time we succeeded in catching him just before he was about to pee or poop. And we'd get him outside in time to praise him for doing his business out on the grass. The other half of the time we'd catch him after he was already in the act or just finished. We stuck his nose in his mess, well not exactly in it, but very close. While we had his nose held down toward his mess, we whopped him a couple times with a rolled up newspaper. When Saturday rolled around Daddy saw that Muffin wasn't housebroken yet. He said to us, "That's it. You've had your chance. Now I'm taking over."

The next time Muffin had an accident in the house, Daddy held Muffin's nose over the poop with one hand and with the palm of his other hand he hit that little puppy so hard his howls filled the entire house. Muffin was shaking like he was hooked up to one of those weight reducing vibrating machines with the belt that goes around your hips that they advertise on TV. Daddy hit him again. Muffin howled even harder. I tried covering my ears, but it didn't help. Daddy hit him just as hard another couple more times, and then he let go. Muffin slinked under our new Danish Modern dining room table. The table Grampa Adams made is now down in the basement with rows of canned peas stacked on it three high. Daddy says when we move from here we're going to get rid of all our old furniture and have all matching furniture.

Kathy, Mary Ruth and I cleaned up Muffin's mess. When we were done, our puppy was still trembling under the table, tail so far between his legs you wouldn't know it was even there. Daddy told us to leave him alone. When Muffin decided to venture out from the table, he went straight to Daddy, who was reading the *Chicago Tribune* in his reclining chair. Daddy ignored him, but Muffin stayed there curled up right by the chair.

Muffin had two more accidents that weekend, and Daddy did the same thing to him. With the last one I was only about five feet away. I couldn't move a muscle when the beating was going on. I know it didn't last that long, but it seemed like forever that I was watching Daddy towering over our trembling puppy slamming him hard with his hand. The squealing was unbearable. I didn't want to be there watching Muffin get swatted. He was only maybe about twice as big as Daddy's palm at that point. But by the end of the weekend, Muffin was house trained, completely. Now if Muffin has a choice of who to be with, Daddy's always his first choice. I wonder why Muffin likes Daddy best because the rest of us are so much nicer to him. But I figure, based on the results, it's just one of those times when Daddy really knows what he's doing,

Muffin chews things, even though he's past the teething stage. This doesn't set Daddy off the way his soiling the house did though. I made Daddy a leather wallet for Father's Day using a leather kit I got last Christmas. It was real pretty, and I did a neat job sewing the pieces together. It was cowhide with big spots of dark brown on a very light brown. And it was soft. Muffin chewed it all up right on Father's Day. Daddy had left it on the floor in its box by his chair. Daddy was sad, I could see that, and so was I, but he didn't beat Muffin over it. I guess wallet chewing isn't as bad as house pooping. I'm still sad about that wallet.

Mommy was afraid when it came to caring for Muffin that she'd have to do all the work, but all she does is let him out every morning around 6 a.m. because he gets rambunctious and needs to run. He likes to chase rabbits and run loose with the other dogs that get let out early and run in a big pack. There's a Great Dane, a German shepherd, a yellow Lab, a St. Bernard, a spotted white and gray mutt with wispy hair, a spaniel of some sort, and Muffin. Those are the regulars in the pack. Muffin's the smallest one, but he's tough. None of the other dogs gets in his way.

Around 7 a.m. Muffin is back, scratching at the front door, hungry for breakfast. That's the other thing Mommy does for him. She feeds him. Well, sometimes if we beg, she'll let us scoop his Gravy Train into his bowl and run some hot water over it to make gravy. But most of the time she wants to do that herself.

Every now and then Muffin doesn't come back from his run, and one, two, or sometimes all three of us girls take his leash and go looking for him. We always find him running with the pack. He teases us for a while, running away just as we're about to grab him and attach his leash to his collar. After a while he lets us catch him, maybe because he knows home is where his food is. After he's eaten, right before it's time to leave for school one of us walks him on his leash, even though he's already had a good run. We take turns walking him again when we get home from school, and then again just before bed time. Muffin has so much energy he needs all the walking we can provide for him.

We have a choke chain collar on him because he pulls so hard on his leash. If he sees a rabbit, he pulls whichever one of us is on the end so hard we get dragged along until we finally lose our grip. He bolts so fast, like nothing I've ever seen. No person can come close to running like he does. Inside we're always playing with him too. We've taught him to sit, lie down, speak (which for him is really a long howl like a wolf), shake hands (paw) and roll over. Lately we've been working on getting him to jump through small hula hoops, the kind we spin on our arms after we get the big ones going around our hips. He's not afraid to jump through the hoops at all. He's so smart we figure we can teach him other fancy tricks and maybe someday get him on the *Ed Sullivan Show*. Then maybe even Mrs. Garnier will like him. Mrs. Garnier has a house full of boys, and she raises poodles. You'd think with all those sons she'd have German Shepherds like Rin Tin Tin, but they're stuck with poodles. When we got Muffin Mrs. Garnier said to me, "Get rid of that stupid dog. You should have one of my poodles. I don't know why you didn't come to me. There's no better pet than a poodle."

I didn't know what to say, other than I love Muffin, and I wouldn't trade him for all the poodles in the world. Besides I think poodles look pretty dumb the way they're clipped, practically shaved completely in some parts and little tufts of curly hair sticking out at the end of their tail and on their legs. They look like clowns to me. Sometimes I see Lyle Garnier, who is a year older than me, walking one of those poodles on a pink or blue leash with rhinestone studs, and I feel sorry for him, especially since Walter and Bonnie from next door told me Lyle likes me.

Ever since they said that, I've been thinking about Lyle when I go outside to play. I'm at a loss as to what to do. Sometimes he'll be down the block tossing a ball around with his brothers. I can tell sometimes he's looking at me, and sometimes I'm looking at him too. Sometimes we'll all join a group in the street for a game of bounce or fly. He and I will be standing just a few feet apart, but not saying anything. One time we all played purple circle. When Lyle traced a circle on my back with the tip of his finger he did it real slow. It made me giggle. After that we set up a relay race. Lyle asked me to be on his team. I said yes. But right at the start of the first relay he pulled a muscle in his leg and limped home. I haven't seen him since and I don't much care. I'm not really interested in boys. I've heard that some kids, when they get to be twelve, they go to parties where they pair off and sit around and kiss. That sounds really boring to me.

So, this interest from Lyle isn't something I would bother to change if I could, but it's also not something that's made my life better than I ever imagined it could be. It's all the great things that have been going on in my family. Mommy and Daddy are even talking about taking us to California next year, that is, if we're not in Italy by then. So, at the moment I'm feeling like the luckiest girl alive.

Down and up, up and down, pace, pace the hallway. Stop at our bedroom where Hank sleeps. Keep the door closed. He might wake up, tell me to come to bed, wrap me in his arms, his crushing, loving arms. Don't go in. Down and up, up and down, shuffle, shuffle. Pass the stairs. Don't lean over the banister. A fall would wake them all.

Stop at the bathroom. Go in. Look in the mirror. Put on the red, red lipstick, so sultry,. Smear it on my lips. Smear it on my cheeks. Rub it, rub it, rub it in. Look at the hair sticking out. Who is that looking at me? Is she drooling? I do not drool. I am the Virgin Mary with a husband and three little girls.

Pull out the rosary, pace, pace, say your prayers. Don't think. Down and up, up and down, pace, pace through the night. Pause at the girls' door. Don't go in. Do not go in. They cringe when the crucifix grazes their skin as I lean over, praying to save their souls. This is how I spent my last nights in the world.

Mary Agnes

Daddy

I love Daddy's robe. It's silky soft and cranberry colored with gray lapels and cuffs on the sleeves, and it has a nice thick matching belt that he cinches around his waist. And if I think about his robe, I can't help but think about his slippers too. They are nice dark brown leather slip-ons, worn soft from years of shuffling down the hall to the dining room on Saturday and Sunday mornings—just on weekend mornings—because there's no time for padding around in slippers and robes during the week, unless Daddy's sick, which he is right now—so sick that he's at Little Company of Mary hospital.

Mommy's there at his bedside now. She goes every day. During the week she scoots off when we're at school, and on weekends she leaves in the afternoon. Kathy, Mary Ruth and I occupy ourselves by doing homework, drawing or playing cards and stuff like that. Today, Mommy's cousin Violet is here with us, which is really strange, and stranger still is that Violet invited Walter, from next door, inside. I don't know how that happened. All of a sudden there he was, sitting himself down, big as you please, at our baby grand. He's trying to play *Moonlight Sonata*. Mommy would probably have a cow if she found out. She never lets us invite neighborhood kids inside. It's a huge no-no to even ask. But I didn't let him in, so why should I worry? Soon Daddy will be home, puttering around here in his robe for a couple weeks before returning to work, and that makes me happy because I'll see more of him, even though I feel bad that he's been sick.

On workdays Daddy's usually in and out of the bathroom before I'm out of bed. Then he dresses in his baggy pants and shirt and tie before I'm through eating breakfast. He pulls out of the driveway in his white Ford Galaxy, and sometimes it's still dark outside. If it's winter, the snow on the ground twinkles so beautifully in the glow of the streetlight when he drives off. And if it's one of those rare times when it's dark out, and snow is falling lightly too, there's nothing quite like that in the world. It was like that one Christmas Eve after Kathy, Mary Ruth and I were done with the supper dishes, and we were waiting for Daddy and Mommy to carry our presents—all wrapped in green, red and gold patterned paper—from their bedroom closet to the Christmas tree in the living room. We always open our presents on Christmas Eve for no reason other than that's the way Daddy and Mommy like to do it. I looked out the dining room window and thought those gleaming snowflakes caught falling in the streetlight's beam were fairy tale magic come to life, especially since there wasn't even one set of footprints to mar the blanket of sparkles they made when they landed on the ground. When we move, I hope there's a streetlight near our yard.

Sometimes Daddy wears more casual clothes to work, like the soft gray- and green-toned clothes he wears on weekends, when he's sawing and hammering, always working on something. He says, "There's no end to the work your mother finds for me to do here," as he heads to his basement work area. But even I know that's not really how it is; the work he does around here is work he's decided to do; Mommy can't boss him around, and she can't boss me around when I'm helping him either. Sometimes I put a pencil behind my ear like he does. He'll take his tape measure from his pocket, unfold it, lay it out across a board, and point to where he wants me to draw a little mark. I take my pencil from behind my ear, stick the tip in my mouth to wet it a little bit, and then mark a great big dot right where he says. I tried sawing a board once too, but it was taking me so long back and forth, back and forth with the saw across the wood, and it wasn't nice and even either. I kept getting the teeth of the saw stuck so I had to lift it up and start over.

After a while Daddy got tired of watching me and he took over and, bam, the board was in two pieces in two strokes. He held up the pieces of wood and said, "Someday, Laura, when you're stronger you'll be able to saw just fine. But, you know when we move, we'll have a house that's already finished, so maybe you and I won't need to do any sawing at all. Then what will you do?"

"Help you practice golf?" I asked.

"There you go. Maybe you could even learn how. Would you like that?"

"I don't know."

Daddy's learning how to play golf. He says it's one of the things executives do. He has a set of clubs, and he practices his drives out in the backyard. I chase the balls and bring them back to him. When he practices putting in the side yard, I just watch. I don't know if he's any good at this golf thing yet, but I know he'll get good because he always gets good at the things he does. That's just how it is.

Daddy doesn't know if we're going to Italy for a while before moving to the Northfield area or whether we're going straight to Northfield. It seems the longer things are up in the air, the more Mommy doesn't want to move at all. She says she really wants to stay close to Uncle Jack and Aunt Dorothy. And she says if we get a new house, that is if we absolutely have to move, it'll have to be a ranch house. "I have to be able to keep an eye on those girls, Hank," she says. "Just imagine what they would do left to themselves out of hearing range."

But Daddy just says, "We'll see." He knows we want an upstairs and downstairs, and our own rooms. Wow, to have my own room—that would be something. I'd have time to myself. But all that's on hold for a while until Daddy gets better. He's hardly ever been sick before this and has missed work only a couple of times that I know of. He was sick one day last year, and it was a treat for me because we had a special lunch together. Mommy had a doctor's appointment for her back that had been hurting her a lot, so Daddy was in charge when I came home for lunch.

It was just him and me. He cooked scrambled eggs. Now, eggs I love, but I hardly ever get to eat them. "They're too expensive," Mommy says. But Daddy can override her whenever he wants. We were real peaceful and happy having lunch just him and me. He didn't even quiz me on my addition and subtraction, division or multiplication. See, I'm not up to par. I don't exactly know how he found out, but it was a big deal a few years ago, him getting flash cards because I wasn't up to par. Kathy and Mary Ruth didn't need flash cards, and he didn't say it, but somehow I just knew that I wasn't supposed to need them either. It's like it was an insult to him when he came home with them and took them out of the bag. He had a look on his face like I was maybe about to force him to drink pee. I could tell he was exasperated just holding those cards in his hands before he even said a word. He started flashing them at me like you're supposed to do and asking, "What's the answer to this, Laura? And this? And this?" I got the first few right even though my throat was dry and I was scared. They were easy. 4 + 4, 5 + 2, and 9 + 1. Whew! I was probably all red in the face too as I squeaked out eight, seven and ten because I was feeling guilty that Daddy had to go through this at all. Then he held up 8 + 6. There was a long pause. I just didn't know the answer. Then he said "Eight plus six, Laura. What is eight plus six?"

I was still blank, and so he said it louder, "Eight plus six, Laura. What is eight plus six?"

I wasn't sure what was coming next, whether this was a punishable offense not knowing what eight plus six is. Then he turned the card around for me to see. He did it real slow and deliberate, and said "See, Laura, it's fourteen. Eight plus six is fourteen. You should know that."

I just stood there. He glared at me and said, "Get out of my sight." Then he picked up the paper, and I ran to my bed. That was the end of the flash cards, but I always remember now that eight plus six is fourteen, in case he asks me again, because you never know when Daddy's going to start quizzing you. It could be state capitols, it could be the members of the President's cabinet, it could be math—word problems are the worst—and it's not good to get the answers wrong. It upsets him so much. But the lunch we had together last year was different. He didn't ask me much of anything except how I liked the eggs, and I tasted them, and they were strange because he put Worstershire sauce in them.

Daddy likes to call Worstershire sauce "What's this here sauce." He puts it in lots of stuff. He doesn't cook often, but when he does, it is always a treat. Lima beans, now, they are pretty bland, but not when he spices them up with ketchup, mustard, garlic, minced onion, pepper, Worstershire sauce, Allspice, and any other spice within reach that catches his fancy. Then he bakes them 'til they're dark, dark brown on the top and at the edges. Ummm they're good!

Once he cooked fruit cocktail, and Mommy just kept saying "My heavens, Hank, my heavens," because Daddy took it from the oven and brought it to the table with a dish towel on top of it. Then with a flourish, like a magician, he took the towel off, and there it was all steaming. The juice was a deep brown and the grapes were all puckered like fingers and toes that have been in bath water a long time. It was just not in the realm of normal, and Mommy wasn't sure any of us should eat it. But we did eat it, even though it tasted like something a person really shouldn't be eating. But I loved it anyway because all of Daddy's cooking is a wonderful sort of strange, just like the mural on the dining room wall we all painted before we left for Florida.

I was afraid once we got back from Florida and school started in September, we'd have to paint over all of our brilliant colors, the gray-brown pelican, pink flamingoes, palm trees, mountains in brown, rust and orange, the fluffy clouds. But it turns out that Mommy and Daddy love showing it off to visitors who come to dinner. So I think the mural is here to stay as long as we are. I would love to be eating my eggs with Daddy right there by the mural again. I don't expect him to cook anything for me when he comes back from Little Company of Mary though. He'll have to rest before he can even think of cooking up any of his concoctions. My Uncle Jim O'Neill is Daddy's doctor at Little Company of Mary, not Dr. Frank, our doctor in Hinsdale.

Mommy doesn't much like anything having to do with the O'Neills, so I was surprised when all of a sudden Uncle Jim became Daddy's doctor. Even though Mommy sucks in her breath and scowls if we mention any of them, we still get together with the O'Neills from time to time, like not too long ago we were all at Uncle Jim's for Grampa's 80th birthday. And Grampa still comes to take us to dinner for our birthdays. He brings a whole jar full of pennies for the birthday girl, even though Mommy won't take us to Riverview anymore. That's how we always used to spend our pennies from Grampa. She says the park's really gone down hill and there are people there that she doesn't want us mixing with. It was as fun as ever last time we went a couple of years ago, but with Mommy, I guess, having fun doesn't really matter.

Sometimes we even get to stay with Grampa O'Neill for a day or two. Once we even got to stay an entire week. That's when Mommy had a miscarriage. Only a few days before she lost her baby, the three of us were at the dining room table with Daddy. Mommy was in the kitchen, just starting to cook supper. He asked Kathy and Mary Ruth, "So girls, how would you like to replace Laura with a baby?"

Neither one of them said anything. They just looked into his eyes, trying to figure out if he was joking.

"Wouldn't you like that, to replace Laura?"

I was starting to feel mighty uncomfortable with this line of questioning. What if they said they wanted to replace me? I wondered where I would go.

Kathy said, "I wouldn't want to replace Laura with some strange new baby."

"Yeah," Mary Ruth added, "At least with Laura, we know what we've got."

Then Daddy called to Mommy, "The girls don't want a baby brother or sister, Helen. What do you think of that?"

Kathy said, "We didn't say that. You asked us about replacing Laura with a baby. That's different."

"Yeah," Mary Ruth declared. "You shouldn't . . ." She couldn't finish her sentence. Tears were welling in her eyes. She was really upset. Daddy leaned in over Mary Ruth, so close I knew she could feel his breath on the top of her head. "I shouldn't what, Mary Ruth?" he demanded.

My stomach started to churn. Daddy doesn't usually say we've said things we haven't said. I was afraid he was starting to adopt Mommy's ways. Then Mommy came from the kitchen. "What did they say?" she asked.

"Oh, nothing, dear. I was just joking. Should we tell them now?"

"May as well," she said.

"Well, girls, you're going to have a new baby brother or sister soon."

"Really? When?" Kathy asked.

"Oh, just under four months," Mommy said.

"Wow," I said. "Where will the baby sleep?"

"With the three of you," Daddy replied. This was before Grampa Adams died. That night we talked for quite a while about where a crib could possibly fit in our room. There wasn't any available floor space. We were stumped. But then that same week, we were shipped off to Grampa O'Neill's. We didn't know that Mommy was having a miscarriage. Daddy told us a week later when we got home.

Mommy says I act different when I come back from Grampa's. She doesn't like it one bit. And I think maybe that's why we go there so seldom. So I was surprised that Daddy went to Uncle Jim for help when he got sick because I don't think Daddy and Uncle Jim even like each other much. Plus we have a hospital nearby that's supposed to be outstanding, and we have a family doctor here, Dr. Frank. We hardly ever see him, partly because my grampa's a doctor too. He can get us just about any medicine for free and do the school check-ups when we need them. Another reason we don't see Dr. Frank much is because Mommy says he's a butcher. Personally, I think he's really nice. He took care of me the Halloween in second grade when I fell from the top bar of the jungle gym. I slipped when I was doing a flip. I banged myself up all the way down to the ground and broke my wrist—three fractures and two cracks.

After I fell, Mommy gave me a good tongue-lashing. Then she sat me on the living room couch, sprayed Bactine on my wrist and wrapped a rag around it. "There. That'll be fine," she said.

I sat there for a long time as darkness crept into the room.

I was worried because my wrist was fatter than usual and the little knobby bone on the outside was sticking up really far. I knew this wasn't an ordinary sort of bump, and I was so scared I was shivering. It hurt so bad if I tried to move my arm or hand, or even my fingers a teeny tiny bit. And Grampa Adams got it in his head to quiz me about which wrist was hurt. I'd always had trouble telling right from left, and he and Mommy loved to trip me up on that. But I'd realized that I could always tell my right hand from my left if I looked at my thumbs because my right thumb has a scar from where Rusty bit me. I couldn't move my left thumb, but I moved the other one to get a good look. It had the scar, so I knew, for sure, it was my left wrist that was hurt, and I told him so. He told me I was wrong to see if I'd change my mind, but I didn't. Then he insisted that I try to move my left arm, saying that I was just faking that it hurt so bad.

Finally Daddy came home from work, took one look at my wrist and rushed me to the emergency room. After I got patched up, I saw doctor Frank every couple of weeks so he could check on my progress. And while my wrist was healing, Daddy made Mommy learn to drive in case of emergencies. Then he got her a spanking new, red and white Chevy, and that's how we got to my last appointment with Dr. Frank.

At that last checkup, Dr. Frank lifted me off the exam table and declared my wrist good as new. "Just don't go flying off any jungle gyms anymore," he said. I was so happy I thought I'd skip around the room. But Mommy grabbed my wrist and said, "Now, Laura, settle down. You know your wrist is never going to be normal. If I told you once I told you a thousand times, it's going to hurt when it's damp for the rest of your life. Oh, yes indeed, it'll be painful, like rheumatism, but that won't be so bad because then you'll be able to tell everyone when it's going to rain." Then she turned to Dr. Frank and said with a little laugh, "Right, Doctor?"

Dr. Frank knitted his frost-white eyebrows together and said, "Why fill the child's head with such thoughts? As far as I know, her wrist is going to be just fine from here on in." I knew right then and there I was with Dr. Frank on that one.

All the time my wrist was healing we were learning cursive writing in school. We started November 1st, the day after Halloween. So I had to learn cursive with my right hand, and Mommy says I was writing more with my left hand before that. She said to Dr. Frank, "What about her having to learn to write with her right hand? Surely that's going to cause her problems down the road, Doctor."

But Dr. Frank said, "Honestly, I think it's okay. If she wants to write with her left hand she can just switch back." I haven't wanted to switch, not yet anyway. I got used to writing cursive with my right hand right away. I think I've always written more with my right than my left. It's just now I don't use my left hand for writing at all, and I used to. So I don't think Dr. Frank is a butcher like Mommy says. But when Daddy first went into the hospital she told us, "Uncle Jim is going to take care of your father without an operation. That Dr. Frank, he wanted to cut him right up. Couldn't wait to get his hands on him. Well, I tell you, your father doesn't cotton to being chopped up. Would you? Imagine having your colon chopped out when you don't have to have it done."

Now it's been six weeks since Daddy went to Little Company of Mary. Six whole weeks. And he wound up

173

having not one but two operations. Mommy says they were a success, but ever since the first one we've been praying for Daddy every day at the dining room table. I don't get it. The only times we've ever prayed are when we say grace before meals, at bed time when we do the now-I-lay-me-down-to-sleep prayer, and occasionally when we go to mass, which is maybe four times a year. We've had to pretend that we're being good Catholics when we're around the O'Neills. Sometimes at family gatherings somebody will make a reference to something religious, assuming I know what they mean. I clench all up inside, and I suspect everybody can see right through to my ignorance.

Now, this whole praying thing seems like an even bigger mess to me. After all these years of pretending, we're supposed to mean it when we put our palms together, close our eyes, and bend our heads down. Here we are every day at the dining room table, leaning on our elbows, praying all these Our Fathers and Hail Marys. I know, and probably everybody else knows, that I don't really have a clue what praying is, or what good it will do, or why we need to do it for Daddy right now, especially because Mommy says that Daddy's doing fine and he's coming home any day now.

I've sent Daddy a few cards. I think that will make him happy. I'm not sure though, because I'm not allowed to call. When I asked to call him, Mommy said, "Now Laura, you know it's a toll call, and besides, it would bother him. He's not supposed to be bothered by children right now." I'm not allowed to visit either. "Hospital rules," Mommy says. "You have to be thirteen to get in. Children are such a nuisance at times like this." I don't understand why Kathy can't visit.

She's thirteen, but Mommy will get mad if I ask about that. It must be that Kathy would bother him too, even though she's thirteen.

Mrs. Dearden next door asked the other day, "How's your father, Laura." There was a very serious look in her eyes. These grown-ups. They're always so serious.

I said, "He's fine. He'll be home soon." That's just what Mommy told me. It's what I tell all the neighbors when they ask about him. They're all starting to ask questions about him, maybe because it's been so long since any of them has seen him pull his Galaxy out of the driveway. It seems that everyone on the block wants to see him come home soon.

Mommy's been gone an extra long time today. I guess it's been okay having Violet here keeping us company. Of all the Downers Grove Rusas, she's the nicest one as far as I can tell. She looks me in the eye and asks me how I am like she means it. Of course, I know better than to reply anything other than "fine" to Violet, her being a grown-up and all. Violet is in the kitchen now, and something's sizzling on the stove—smells like meat. She spoke to Mommy a little while ago while I was playing with one of my old cars on the rug. Then she started cooking. I think that may be a first because nobody but Mommy has ever cooked a thing in our kitchen before, except for Daddy every now and then doing one of his Worstershire experiments.

When Violet was on the phone, Walter took a break from the piano keys and started taunting us. "I can play piano better than your mother," he said.

"Can not," Mary Ruth, Kathy and I all insisted.

"Can too. She's not really that good,"

"She's a lot better than you," Kathy said.

That went on for some time back and forth until Violet told us all to cut it out. I was still upset. The idea that he can play better than Mommy, who was once a guest soloist with the Chicago Symphony Orchestra and who gets everyone's complete attention when she plays. No way Walter can do that to people.

So I wish he would go, saying stuff like that. It's time for every kid on the block to be home for supper anyway. It's dark outside. I see headlights coming in the driveway. It must be Mommy. I rush to the door along with Kathy and Mary Ruth. We stand ready to greet her and find out when Daddy will be home. I hope it's tomorrow. The door opens, and here are Gramma and Uncle John. I wonder what they're doing here so late on a Sunday. Gramma comes in, leaning heavily on a cane, and sobbing, she says, "How can you play the piano when you'll never see your father again? Oh, my son, my son."

Walter stops playing. I wonder what Gramma could possibly mean and why she's so upset. Uncle John guides her to a chair by the door. Then he looks at us. His eyes are bloodshot, his beautiful blue eyes, and his face is so, so ashen and sad. He says, "Girls, your father is dead."

At this moment I want him and Gramma to just back up, like a film going backwards. I want them to come in again and stop talking this horrible nonsense about Daddy. Daddy can't be dead. He's too alive. I mean he dances around the house. He runs, he bellows, he's got more oomph than all the other dads on the block combined. He can't be dead. No way. But now I hear Kathy screaming, "No, no, no!" and she runs down the hall to her room. Uncle John races after her.

Mommy's inside the door now, being escorted by my big, huge, grown-up cousin George. She's limping something awful, and trembling. He's got her by the arm, and he helps her get seated at a dining room chair. They don't say anything to Mary Ruth and me, and we don't say anything to them. What is there to say? All I'm thinking is dead, not dead. Daddy is not dead.

Tears are streaming down my face. I look at Mary Ruth, and tears are streaming down her face too. George grabs some Kleenex from the counter near our bright yellow phone and hands us each one piece as Walter slips quietly out the door. Gramma is bent over looking down at her lace-up orthopedic black shoes. One of her tears splashes silently onto the beautiful blue flower pattern of her dress. She rubs her face with the back of her grizzled hand.

Mary Ruth and I sit down on the living room couch where it is dark and quiet. Could it have only been just minutes ago that we were here arguing with Walter? It already seems like ages ago. I remember last year when we had the couch folded out into a bed because all of us had the flu at the same time. We all slept in the living room. Kathy, Mary Ruth and I had milky white medicine. Mommy and Daddy had something darker. I was uncomfortable, but I was also really happy that we were there all together, recovering, all five of us. Now it's Mary Ruth and me, just the two of us, Kleenex all soggy now, wadded up in yellow balls in our fists. But we keep using it and using it and using it. The adults, except for Uncle John, who is with Kathy, are all in the dining room now. I can't stop thinking this can't be true. I can't stop staring at the Kleenex and rolling it around and around in my hand. I can't stop thinking Daddy's going to walk through the door any minute and set everything right. But now Violet says, "Supper's ready. Come and get it."

I can't believe it. We're actually going to eat supper? Quietly, Mary Ruth and I move toward the table. Mommy, Gramma, George and Violet are already seated. I sit down in George's shadow. Uncle John and Kathy come in. And now we all bow our heads. Together we say grace. "Bless us oh Lord and these thy gifts which we are about to receive..." I think any Lord who takes my Daddy away is not a Lord I want to pray to, talk to, think about. I clench my teeth. The food is passed around. George puts a hamburger on my plate. I put mustard and ketchup on the bun, not on the burger. Daddy says you never put condiments on the meat, always put it on the bread, and it's best to do what Daddy says. People are talking quietly, but not to me. They all seem so far away now, like I'm in an incubator, not ready to come out to be part of this. I take a bite of the hamburger. It was cooked too fast, so inside it's raw. Raw. I hate raw hamburger, absolutely hate it. I put it down and stare at my plate.

"Not hungry, Laura?" Uncle John asks. I can't answer. I can't make a sound. I just shake my head in response.

Mommy says, "Now Laura, Violet went to the trouble to cook us this meal. You'd just better start eating," but I can't move my hand from my lap to pick up the food.

I look up at Uncle John. He looks at Mommy and says, "Maybe it's okay, Helen, to waste a little food today."

And she darts him a look like she's not happy with what he said, but she doesn't say anything.

I still can't speak. I don't care if I ever eat again. I'll probably get this raw hamburger for breakfast tomorrow. But I don't care. I listen half-heartedly as bits of conversation float around and around in my mind. "The second operation. That awful second operation. He was just too weak to survive it. He should have had the first operation right when Dr. Frank said, when he was stronger, when he was stronger. You know, he walked into that hospital all by himself, all by himself, on his own two legs, and now they're gonna carry him out. He was strong as you and me when he walked in there, strong as you and me. Hank would never have wanted to live like that, like that, having one of those bags, those colostomy bags. I can't even imagine it. Why didn't someone find out what he was saying this afternoon? His lips were moving at the end. He was trying to tell us something. He was trying to tell us something, tell us something, tell us something. Now we'll never know. We'll never know."

Then I hear George saying my name. I look at his long, sober face, "You know, Laura, I lost my dad when I was just thirteen." I just want to scream: that doesn't help me now, you dummy. I don't care. I don't care when you lost your dad. It's not bringing my Daddy back, is it? Besides I just turned eleven years old. Thirteen seems ancient to me. I'd give anything to have Daddy even for just another two years. Just leave me alone. You don't know me. You don't know how I feel.

But I stay quiet. I know he means well. I stare down at the hamburger oozing blood onto its bun. Violet gets up to begin clearing the table.

"Girls, get up now and help Violet," Mommy says.

Violet says, "It's okay, Helen. I'll do it. There'll be plenty for the girls to do after this, besides it's getting late. They're probably tired."

Then Mommy turns and looks with her fierce brown eyes from Kathy to Mary Ruth and then to me, and she says, "Yes, girls you probably are tired. Better get ready for bed. You've got school tomorrow."

I get up from the table, thinking that maybe she'll have mercy; maybe just this once she'll change her mind. But it doesn't happen. There's no use arguing with Mommy once her mind is made up.

Morning creeps up like an upset stomach, and pretty soon I'm a zombie trudging to school. I don't understand why somebody—Gramma, Uncle John, George, Violet— couldn't have said that maybe it would be better for us not to go to school today. Have any of them stopped to think that it might be hard to face everybody, the teachers, the books, the chalkboards, the kids—all of it? It doesn't feel like I'm ever going to smile again. I want so much to just sit down somewhere, to not have to talk to anybody, to be still as long as I need to. But I'm trudging along with Kathy and Mary Ruth on this windy, damp Monday. November 6, 1960. Daddy's been dead less than twenty-four hours. It was yesterday at 3:05 p.m. that he breathed his last.

It seems completely wrong that everything in the world around us should be so normal as we make our way to Hinsdale Junior High School. The cool wind, the cloudy sky, the cars driving by slowly, parents and kids in their usual morning routines while my heart is blacker than the coal that used to gleam in Gramma's basement. Kathy says she cried all night last night. I cried some too talking to God, asking him to please undo this, make it all a big mistake. All these memories of Daddy kept flashing through my mind, starting from when he walked through Gramma's door the day Uncle Dean dropped me off there. I ran to him, and he scooped me up into the air. My memories end with the last time I saw him at home in his robe and slippers. I just get sadder with each memory, knowing that this is it, that's all I'm ever getting of him.

When I fall asleep I dream that I am at a party in a corner by myself, facing the wall. A cool wind swirls all around me, but everybody else is laughing, throwing confetti in the air, having a great time. Then somebody leans in close to me and says, "Laura, your father's here." And the cool wind just disappears. I feel happier than I ever have. In an instant I go from shriveling up inside to just glowing with joy. I turn around, and through the crowd, at the entrance to the room, I get a glimpse of his dark hair, his sparkling gray eyes, his smile. I make a dash for him. But the room is so crowded, it's hard to get by all the people milling about. I push and get bumped backward, but I push on. I get closer and closer calling out, "Daddy, Daddy, it's me, Laura." And then when I am almost there, almost about to touch the sleeve of his crisp, white dress shirt, I wake up. Oh, I wake up, and I wish I never had because what I feel is the same thing hitting me, the realization that he is dead. It creeps all over me just like yesterday when I first got the news.

Seeing Daddy now is the only thing in the world I want. I'd give up my right hand. I'd give up both of my hands, my feet, my voice, everything just to see him again. The one thing in the world I want, I'll never get.

Anything I was ever mad at him about, any punishment I didn't think I deserved, none of it matters. None of it compares to the fact that he's never going to walk through the front door again. He's never again going to smile down on me and call me Shimp. I'm mad too. Why is it my daddy who died? Nobody else's daddy is gone. Every last one of the kids at school—their lives are going on as they were, and mine is changed forever. Why?

I wonder what I'm going to do at school. How much does Mommy think I'm going to learn today? I'm never going to feel the same about Sunday again because it's on Sunday that God took my daddy away. And now Monday is here, and I'm never going to feel the same about Monday either. Kathy, Mary Ruth and I are at the corner where they turn to the side of the building where the seventh and eighth graders enter. I have one more lonely block to the sixth grade side. It's in the old part of the building that I thought was beautiful until today.

"Goodbye," I say to them.

"Bye. See you later," they say.

"Yeah. See you later."

And I'm on my own. The wind is picking up, and the beautiful brown, golden orange and red autumn leaves swirl around my feet. I'm walking slower the closer I get to the turn-off to the school grounds. And now, here I am. I need to turn left. I see my classmates, moving, laughing, huddling in groups here and there. The bell hasn't rung yet. I wait, partly concealed by a bush near the walk, for the bell to ring. Then after everyone has lined up and gone in the doors, after they're all inside, I go to the door, open it, and walk up the three flights of stairs to where the sixth-grade classes are held. In my coat pocket I have a note from Mommy to my homeroom teacher. I have it memorized. "Dear Miss Tanner, Laura will be unable to attend school Tuesday, November 7, through Thursday, November 9, due to the death of her father. Sincerely, Helen E. Gross." I guess that means I'll be right back here again Friday too.

Upstairs I stop at my locker and put my turquoise and black car coat inside. I'm wearing my favorite outfit, the one Daddy got me in fourth grade. It's a little shorter on me than it was, but it still fits fine. I hope I never outgrow it. I walk into the classroom and hand Miss Tanner the note. She reads it, looks up and trains her eyes right on my face. And just as quickly as a marshmallow bursts into flame when you hold it over the fire too long, tears just explode from my eyes. And what does she do? She hugs me. She puts her long arms around me and hugs me soft and slow. I start to sob, only I hold the noise in so I'm just heaving. She holds me there for a while, forgetting about the classroom full of kids milling about. Nobody at my house, not even Gramma, has hugged me since I got the news that Daddy died, and I just break apart, all the while I'm trying to hold myself together. The tears just keep coming. I've gotten Miss Tanner's robin's-egg blue mohair sweater wet right above her breasts, breasts so beautiful like Sophia Loren that they make all the boys in class hold in giggles when she walks by.

Finally I stop the sobs. Miss Tanner gives me some Kleenex, and I walk to my desk, squishing the wet tissue in my hand. This boy Raymond who sits near me asks another boy Augie who also sits nearby, "What's wrong with her?" Augie says, "Her father died." Just hearing this makes me start crying again, harder than when Miss Tanner was hugging me. I wonder how Augie knows my Daddy died. I start sobbing out loud. I try to stop, but I can't. Miss Tanner comes to my desk, takes me by the hand, and leads me out the door, down the hall, and to the stairwell I just walked up several minutes before. She says for me to stay there for a while until I feel ready to come back to class.

So I sit on the cold stairs, looking out the window to the empty playground, the leaves still swirling around when the wind gusts up. A basketball someone left outside by mistake bumps up against a chain-link fence. I want to throw myself down the stairs, bang myself up really bad, get myself unconscious, anything to get away. After a while I stop crying, and I just sit there, not wanting to go to class, but feeling guilty because I'm not crying anymore so I should probably go. I don't move. I just want this day to not be happening. I want to go home and have everybody say, "It was all a big mistake, Laura, your father's not really dead. The doctors were wrong." That's what I want.

Then our math teacher, Mr. Trout, comes in and asks, "Are you ready to go to class now, Laura?"

I say, "I guess so," since I'm not crying anymore.

I think if I just look around at things, the smooth gray and tan floor tiles, the books on the shelves in class, the lockers, the erasers on their ledges, the words teachers write on the boards, if I can do that and not think about Daddy, maybe I can get through the day without crying again. So I go on.

I keep all the tears inside, making myself dizzy with this effort to keep things down like rotten food, until Tuesday afternoon at Daddy's wake. Sitting on a dusty pink love seat, I still can't believe that he's really gone. Hundreds of people

come to pay their respects—friends, neighbors, relatives, people from Daddy's work. There are 46 different floral arrangements lined up starting from each end of Daddy's open casket and then down the aisles of this musty funeral parlor room. One of the arrangements is from my old Girl Scout troop. I dropped out of Scouts in fifth grade. We were starting to learn camping skills, thing we'd need to go on overnights, and I knew I wouldn't be allowed to go sleep in the woods, plus I was scared to do it anyway. So I quit before I'd have to explain anything to anyone. I thought they'd forgotten all about me, so I was surprised to see everybody's name on the card, even Donna, the girl I dumped so heartlessly in first grade. The troop leader probably made them all sign.

Daddy's wake is in the same room that Grampa Adams' was in last year. Only it's Mommy standing alone at the casket this year, greeting all who come. I keep thinking about how weird that is, and how completely different things are now. I don't know how I'm going to bear living without Daddy. There's only emptiness where he used to be. Just sad, empty space. That's all that's left of me too. Deep, sad, empty space.

Kathy, Mary Ruth and I don't have to stand up with Mommy; she'd just as soon not have us in her hair, she says. But we do have to say hello to everybody who comes up to us and answer questions. I am amazed at how much laughter there is at the wake and how many stupid questions people ask. Like Uncle Jim comes up to Kathy, who is wearing tan tights and asks, "Katherine, are those Supphose?" That's a kind of hosiery that's being advertised on TV a lot. I just glare at him. I am thinking about how Dr. Frank told Daddy he'd have to operate on him right away. Then Uncle

Jim told Daddy he thought he could get him better without an operation. So Daddy checked into Uncle Jim's hospital, and he came out dead. Now Uncle Jim is asking Kathy if she's wearing Supphose? I think maybe he should say, "I'm so sorry your father died, Kathy. I did all I could do to save him," because I'm sure he did do all he could to save him. But he hasn't said anything like that. Nobody has. Not to Kathy, Mary Ruth and me anyway.

Kathy, Mary Ruth and I go into the ladies room just to get away, and Mommy's friend Florence is in there smoking a cigarette, moving her flabby arms that are scarred from an accident she had when her car and a bus collided. She swears the accident was the bus driver's fault. The Chicago Transit Authority says otherwise. Florence grumbles a lot about that. I am trying very hard not to look at her arms when she says, "What are you gals starin' at? Oh, my arms, yeah. They're not a pretty sight. Well, do you think all you should see are pretty sights? Just wait. You think yous have it bad now. Just you wait. I was on my own by the time I was thirteen, Kathy's age. You've been livin' in a fantasy land girls. You're just now getting a little taste of reality. It's about time the three of yous learn what life is really like. This is nothing."

I sure don't know what to say to that. Kathy and Mary Ruth's silence tells me they don't know either. I've never liked Florence. She's always complaining about her alcoholic husband, John, who when he isn't walking in a sleeveless T-shirt to the refrigerator for a beer, he's sleeping. She complains about her son, Billy, too. She grumbles about how it's not fair the condition he's in. She says, "He was born just as smart as the three of yous. You're not so special, you know. He was probably smarter even. And now look at him. John dropped baby Billy on his head before he could walk. Now he's a retard. It could have been any one of yous. Just remember that."

She always directs these complaints to us as though the state of her life is our fault. We watch her in silence in the ladies room as we wash our hands. She takes long puffs on her Pall Mall, tapping her long red fingernails on the almost empty pack. She exhales a big puff of smoke our way and says, "You don't have it bad. This is nothing for you, nothing compared to what Helen is going through, stuck with three girls that aren't even her own. I'd dump you if I was her, but she's a fool. She's got it a lot worse than you do, so do I. Remember that."

We each pull down a paper towel from the dispenser near the sink, wipe our hands really fast, and one, two, three, put the used brown paper into the wastebasket. It is near the black pumps on Florence's swollen feet. We back away and Kathy says, "Well, we've got to get back now, Florence." We all turn and make our escape. She looks settled in, like she plans to spend the rest of the wake right where she is, talking ugly like that to everybody who comes in.

Back in the crowd outside, the weird comments raining down on us from the other adults don't seem as bad anymore. I sit on a bench against a wall where a couple of people I don't know are standing and talking to each other as though they could be at a backyard barbeque. Then Grampa O'Neill walks over and sits down next to me. He doesn't say a word. He just puts his arm around me and leans me into his chest real close. Tears flow out of my eyes across my cheeks and

187

spread onto his clean white shirt, soaking the pocket where he always keeps a fresh Papermate ballpoint pen clipped just so. But that time with Grampa doesn't last long. Pretty soon Uncle Dean walks up and says, "Well, Dad, I think it's about time we hit the road."

Kathy and Mary Ruth plunk down next to me, and we just sit quietly in a row, watching Grampa and Uncle Dean make their way to the door, stopping every so often to talk to one person or another.

I want to be anywhere but at the funeral parlor where my father's body is in a casket for all to view. My mind keeps drifting back to when it was Grampa Adams' body in his casket in this very same room. It was almost a lark back then, a curiosity. Now it is my life being turned upside down, broken apart, and swept away, swept away by God. I am sure he's punishing me now for being so happy when Grampa Adams died. I tried to be sad then, and when I couldn't do that, I tried to hide my happiness.

At the funeral mass my feelings swirl around inside of me, my own private hurricane. Outwardly, I manage to look pretty composed. I've had a lot of practice hiding my feelings in fights with Kathy and Mary Ruth. I learned long ago that you have to be able to get pounded really hard and not show any emotion. If one of them sits on top of me and socks me with her fist, she just hits harder if I cry. But if I look blank or even manage to smile, she gets bored and gets off pretty fast. Looking calm no matter what's happening is pretty much what I do automatically. But right toward the end of the mass, when the big, strong, gray-suited pallbearers lift his coffin and carry him down the aisle and out of the church, the sadness in my heart, the slow heavy steps as they all go down the aisle, the knowing that soon I will have to get up and follow, it all overpowers me, and the tears let loose. I have to hold my breath to stop the flood.

The funeral procession drives right past the junior high school—the sixth grade side. All my classmates are out on the playground for lunch break. We are heading from the mass at St. Isaac's to the freeway. We are going to a place called Queen of Heaven Cemetery. I see all the kids running and talking like normal. I feel so completely separate from all of them, permanently extracted like a rotten tooth from the life I was living just a few days ago.

At the cemetery it starts to rain, a light shower that makes the evergreen nearby extra shiny and the sky extra gray. There are lots of prayers, and finally the coffin goes down, ever so slowly, into the grave. I stare down as Daddy's name in gold letters receives the first shovel of dirt. I want to cry out, "No! Wait! I'm not ready to say good-bye." But I remain silent, just staring at what I can still see of the letters until Unc touches my elbow lightly and says, "It's time to go."

We get back into the hearse and go to a restaurant. Everyone is served a plate of roast beef. I just cut the meat and push the chunks around in the gravy until it is time to go. Then we stand there—Kathy, Mary Ruth, Mommy, Unc, Gramma, and me—under the restaurant awning that protects us from the rain as people say their last good-byes, get into their cars and drive one after another out of the parking lot and for the most part out of our lives.

I'm right about having to go to school on Friday, the day after Daddy's funeral. Kathy, Mary Ruth and I go to classes and pick up all of our make-up work from the wake and funeral days. Mommy expects it to all be done by Monday. Nobody says a word to me about Daddy the whole day in class, or at lunch. Maybe it's better that way. What do they all care anyway, and why would I want to talk about him to people who don't really care?

Jillie comes over from the other sixth grade cycle after school. It's the second time I've talked to her all year. The sixth grade is divided into two groups called cycles. We're on opposite ends of the hall and don't have any of the same teachers. We tend not to mingle with each other. The first time Jillie and I spoke this school year was right after school started. She came up to me and asked, "How is your cycle? Isn't it weird to have all the kids from our old school split up like this?"

'It's kind of fun," I said. "There's so many more kids now."

"Yeah, that's true. Made any new friends yet?"

"Sort of," I said because there was a little group I was hanging out with at lunch time.

"That's good because you know what?"

"What?"

"Becky and Diane and some of the other kids from Madison School in my cycle say they're really glad you're not with us. They say you're a show off, and they hate your stupid jokes. They felt like they always had to laugh at them."

Right then I felt winded, like she'd just slugged me square in the gut. I felt like I was about to throw up the peanut butter sandwich, milk and Fudgesicle I'd had for lunch. It didn't surprise me so much about Diane. I knew she'd pretty much disliked me since first grade, but I had no idea Becky felt the same. I thought she and I got along well. I even thought she liked me. My whole sense of fifth grade changed at that point. If Becky couldn't stand me, I wondered how many other kids couldn't stand me either and just pretended to like me when they were around me. I wanted to go hide somewhere, and I decided that in the future I should steer completely clear of Becky and Diane. I didn't know what to say to Jillie so I just said, "Oh," and I turned and walked away from her.

She followed me and said, "I like you, Laura. I think they're wrong about your jokes."

"I didn't know I told jokes," I said.

"It's not like you tell joke jokes. You just say weird things sometimes. And sometimes you're funny."

I was relieved to hear the bell ring and put an end to our conversation. I hadn't really given Jillie or the other kids in her cycle much thought since that day. And now here's Jillie walking up to me as I stand at my locker and fish some books out. As soon as I spy her, I close my locker door, turn and dash into Mrs. Larkfield's classroom. She's my English teacher. She peers through her bifocals, grading papers at her desk. She looks up when I come in and says, "Hi Laura, do you need help with something?"

"Not really," I say, "May I erase your blackboard?"

"Of course," she says smiling.

I pick up an eraser and start rubbing the board vigorously at one end. It feels pretty good to be doing something so simple as erasing a board. Then Jillie walks in. I can't believe she's followed me into the room. She picks up an eraser and starts working too. Then she starts bumping into me and trying to erase spots I am about to erase just before I get to them, making a game of it. I start to do the same thing to her. She giggles, and for one brief little burst I forget who I am and where I am. I giggle too, but as soon as I hear my laughter in the room I think of Daddy, and I wonder how in the world I can have possibly giggled when he's only been buried a little more than twenty-four hours. I think I must be some kind of moron. I erase the rest of the board quietly, ignoring Jillie. Then I put the eraser down, and walk out of the room.

Jillie follows me, "Want some company on the walk home?" she asks.

"No thanks. I want to be alone," I say. Then I walk into the girls' bathroom and shut myself in one of the stalls until I am sure she is gone.

On Saturday afternoon I sit at the dining room table with Mary Ruth, trying to read my social studies book, and I can't even read one sentence before my mind starts to wander off. I don't know how Mary Ruth is doing with her French homework. It looks like that's what she's working on. Neither of us has a desk, so we always do our homework at the dining room table. Mommy's in the kitchen, pulling out casseroles that neighbors sent over to us during the last week. I think she is deciding which one to serve for supper. Kathy walks in and joins us at the table. Mommy sees the three of us sitting at the table and says, "Now that you're all together I have something to tell you."

"What is it?" Mary Ruth asks.

"Girls, Muffin has to go. We're going to give him away."

"What?" all three of us practically gasp.

"You heard me."

"Why? Why ever would you want to give our dog away?" Kathy asks.

"Because he's too much trouble and expense. I can't handle it now that your father's gone."

Mary Ruth says, "We're the ones who walk him and play with him—"

"That's nothing. I'm the one who gets up at 6:00 a.m. each morning to let him out."

"We'd do that ourselves if you let us get out of bed before you do," Kathy says.

Then Mommy says, "I'm allergic to him anyway. I've been suffering. Are you telling me you want me to suffer?"

"We're not telling you anything. Since when are you suddenly allergic to our dog? You never said anything before," Kathy argues.

"Stop needling me, you girls. You think you're so smart. I've always been allergic to dogs. I just put up with them for my father and then for your father. Now I don't have to anymore."

I suspect that she's making up the whole allergy thing, but I don't want to call her a liar.

"If you'd let us keep him, we could earn money for his keep by baby-sitting. You wouldn't have to buy his food," Kathy suggests.

"I told you girls we're giving the dog away, and that's final. I'm the boss here, and this is my house. The three of you are just here by my good graces, and you'd better get used to it. It's only my good nature that's letting you stay, and when you're 18, you're out, got that? You're out. So in the meantime, what I say goes. We're getting rid of the dog."

A week of desperate wishes for a change in Mommy's heart goes by. Saturday comes again. Uncle John picks up the three of us, and Muffin, and he drives us to Muffin's new home. It's a family with three kids, just like us, but some of them are boys. We take turns just hugging Muffin close in the back seat until Uncle John stops in front of a yellow brick house in a town pretty far from Hinsdale. We stay in the car and watch Unc lead Muffin to the door, each of us hoping until the very last second that Unc will turn around and race with Muffin back to the car. We all look away when the door to Muffin's new home opens. We don't even want a peek at his new family. None of us says one word the whole way home.

A few weeks after that awful drive Mommy sneers while slapping out our creamed-chipped-beef-over-stale-bread supper, "Those people who took Muffin had to give him away. They sent him to a farm because he was so rambunctious. So you see, I was right. Muffin is too much trouble to handle. It's because you girls didn't raise him right."

I don't bother to reply. I figure he could just as easily have been rambunctious because he missed us and wanted to come home. I picture him on the farm chasing rabbits and roaming far and wide like he likes to do and think that might be a good life for him. But, oh, how I miss him—all of his energy, his tricks, running all around the neighborhood. I secretly hope that he runs away from the farm and finds his way back to our front door. If he does, maybe Mommy won't make us give him away again.

Losing Muffin can't compare to losing Daddy. I mean having Daddy gone is like trying to walk blindfolded on stilts across an icy freeway. Life marches on; days lead to weeks; so much has changed. First and most important is just his absence. The space that he used to fill seems to be taken up by evil shadows pressing in on the house, making us all short of breath, pale, listless. A girl only gets one daddy in this life. I would think dealing with that, knowing that the rest of my days he won't be here with me, won't ever look at my report cards again, won't go to my school graduations, won't walk me down the aisle when I get married, won't ever drive me anywhere in the Galaxy again, singing at the top of his lungs—that should be enough. But there's more, so much more it's choking me. Little things and big things just pile up, a big traffic jam in the arteries and veins leading to and from my heart.

One thing is that we're poor now. Mommy says we're living on less than a quarter of what Daddy made this past year, the year after he became an executive and got a raise. She gets $56 a month Social Security for each of us, and $75 for her. That's it. That's got to cover everything from now on. She was offered a job by her old boss Howard Miller, the announcer at WIND radio. She turned it down. It paid $225 per week, but she said that she couldn't possibly leave us to our own devices while she was at work. The matter wasn't open to discussion. That was it. Period. So we're now in a completely different financial bracket than just about everybody else in Hinsdale. I think we should move some place that's not an upper-middle-class community, some place more middle of the road, where there will be people around in a situation similar to ours. But Mommy says she's hanging onto this house for dear life.

All of this is giving our home a desperate feeling, like fires are burning all around the edges of the house, and as soon as we put one out there's another one. It's always smoldering just beneath the surface, not so quickly that we can't put flames out, but quick enough that it's starting to wear us out. And this is just the beginning. I have seven more years to live here like this before I can move on to whatever my future will be.

We never eat at the dining room table anymore, unless we have company, which isn't often. Mommy slaps suppers together for us and slams our plates down on the kitchen counter like it's too much trouble to walk the few extra steps to the dining room table for Kathy, Mary Ruth and me. I guess it was just for Daddy that she went to the effort of having nice meals, not for us.

The food we have, the things we have to put in our mouths now, that's all different too. We used to have regular meals— baked chicken, pot roast, spaghetti for supper, and pancakes on Saturday mornings. All of the meals were burned, but at least they were ordinary. But no more. Mommy finds really strange foods in dented cans, things past their sell dates. She hauls home frozen dinners kind of like TV dinners that are hard to chew and almost tasteless. Even the hot dogs she gets now are these greasy, strange-smelling things. I don't want to complain. I realize we don't have any money. But Mommy seems to take such delight in serving us this crud, watching our reactions with her little cat smile, knowing it's far from pleasing. If we show too strong a reaction she says, "You should be happy there's any food at all." I never used to think much about food, but now sometimes I find myself just daydreaming about a nice ham sandwich with Swiss cheese on rye bread, or a plate full of eggs noodles with round steak and gravy. And it's creepy knowing that kind of food is as scarce in my life as hundred-dollar bills.

The biggest change since Daddy's absence is in Mommy herself. At least before, when Daddy was alive, Mommy did have good moments, times when she was happy and kind to us. But his death really set something loose in her, something that repulses and terrifies me as much as a giant poisonous snake slithering around the house would. She swears, she belches, she screams vulgar things. I don't think Daddy ever saw this side of her. It's like she kept it locked away for his sake, and BAM, as soon as he was gone it all just oozed out. The only time I can be sure she won't be really crass is when someone drops by to visit or if she's on the phone making nice with one of her friends. Then she's all prim and proper. I think people who aren't around all the time think that sweet way she has of being is how she is all the time. They don't know that talking to her can be like getting one electric shock after another.

A couple of days after we had to give Muffin away, I was putting a carton of watered-down milk on the shelf in the refrigerator. Just as I closed the refrigerator door Mommy came up and stood on the opposite side of the kitchen counter from me, near the phone. It was early morning and I had just woken up and was swept silent by sadness because I'd dreamed about seeing Daddy at the party again. I dream that every night now, so every morning I go through first the joy of seeing him and then the aching letdown of waking to reality. So I was trying to pull myself out of that when Mommy looked me up and down and said, "You never loved your father, you heartless, selfish little bitch. I know that. He knew it too, and you know what? He didn't love you either. Ha! He couldn't wait to marry you off when you were sixteen. That's all he thought you were good for, marrying off. So

197

don't you go around thinking you're so damn special. Your own father couldn't wait to be rid of you."

I know I loved my father, and I used to be sure he loved me, but her saying that put a little doubt in my mind. It was like a tiny spot of ink on the cuff of a shirt that you hardly notice, but it's still there. I think about it. What if she's right? What if he really said that? My own father wanting to be rid of me. Maybe he had a vulgar, crass side just like she does, a side they kept hidden from us. How will I ever know for sure? I don't understand the ways of grown-ups. I don't even understand myself. I didn't say anything back to Mommy when she said that about Daddy. I just put the glass of milk I'd poured down on the counter and walked away.

I would like to call Gramma, just to hear her voice. But Mommy won't let me use the phone, not even to call a number in Hinsdale. I asked her the other day if she would call Gramma so we could all talk to her, and she said, "Now Laura, you know that's a toll call, and we simply can't afford to call your grandmother right now." But Mommy calls Gramma whenever she wants. I hear her complaining about us, saying we're driving her crazy and that we don't want to go visit Gramma with her. That's not true, but I'm afraid Gramma believes her. Mommy says, "I had to work hard to get your grandmother to like me. She didn't think I was good enough for your dad and you. Ha! But now she's singing a different tune. She's even apologized to me. She knows, she knows the pain you're putting me through. She knows how ungrateful you are too, how you have no idea how much I'm doing for you or how much she sacrificed for you when you were little, taking on three no good girls like you at her age."

Mommy says other awful things that aren't true too. I came in one day after school. Kathy was already inside sitting at the dining room table drawing a picture of a horse. She loves horses. Mommy was screaming, "You killed your mother. You killed your father, and now you three girls are trying to drive me to the grave inch by inch too." I could see she was just starting to rev up like one of those gospel preachers. When she would stop was anybody's guess. I slinked past Mommy down the hall to Mary Ruth's and my room.

I can't for the life of me figure out what we've done to make Mommy feel like we're trying to kill her. We're trying to be good, trying to be helpful, but she's unhappy with us no matter what we do. Sometimes we meet in Kathy's room to try and figure out how to do a better job of helping Mommy, to let her know we love her. We want to help us be whatever kind of family we can be at this point, the kind of family Daddy would want us to be, but we just go around in circles, no solutions yet.

We tried, my Hank and I. And we failed, failed as a couple, failed as friends, failed as family, as anything, we failed. And the children. What of our girls? Our girls. Who's going to throw them a net or a rose or a kiss when they need it? Hank has already passed on to a better place. He didn't kill himself; he just lost the will to live. That's not a sin. I committed a murder, my own, and I am here still, pacing, pacing on the edge of my daughters' lives, unable to help them, and knowing I will not be released until they forgive me. I have no idea when that will be. They think they never knew me and have nothing to forgive.

Mary Agnes

Plan X

It's Christmas 1962, my third one without Daddy. I'd like to be thinking about peace and joy, but there's something wrong with Mommy. I mean there's something really wrong with Mommy, something besides her usual backaches, her limp, her elbow scratching and foul temper. She had some sort of accident. She won't talk about it, but now the bathtub drain, around the drain, the porcelain is stained a deep brownish red. It bothers me. Every time I come in here. It bothers me. I know it has something to do with being a woman, and a woman like Mommy is something I never want to be.

If I could postpone forever getting my period that would be all right. I don't want to walk through the door to sanitary napkins and belts neatly arranged between my underpants and my barely there pubic hair, for I see only pain in front of me and screaming and loneliness and meanness. There must be some other door, some other entrance, but I don't see it. Oh, how I wish I could have Daddy back just for a moment to ask him. "Please, Daddy, find another door. I don't want to go through this one."

Why can't it be that way? Why can't a dead person just appear every now and then and dispense advice?

The sun shines and icicles dangle from our eaves this Christmas morning. Joyous songs of silver bells, silent stars, and glistening snow blast from a radio on the closet shelf above our warm, winter coats. Yet I linger in our narrow little bathroom staring at the bloodstain, staring and dreading that someday it will be my blood staining some sink or tub or skirt somewhere for other people to see. And Mommy is longing for the blood to be mine.

"You don't know what pain is," she rants so often it barely has an effect anymore. Maybe I don't. Maybe I'm not really living this life. That's actually how I feel. I'm observing myself living this life, but from behind something I can't see. It's like I'm holding my breath to keep from moving ahead. The blood. The misery. The screaming. The scratching. The pacing the hallway back and forth, back and forth, hair all mussed up, completely disheveled. But wait now, was that Mommy, or the Mary Agnes of the O'Neills mommy who at one time was Mommy, but just took a rope and stopped it all, all the pain, forevermore. Which Mommy is the pacer in the hallway? I think it was the O'Neill one. This one's a limper and a screamer, not really a pacer.

I look at the blood. I do not yet have my period. Not me. Not me. Is it the change of life for Mommy? I've heard her whisper about it to Florence on the phone, but when I get close enough to actually hear what she's saying, she hushes up and scolds me, "This is none of your beeswax, Laura. Go outside."

She is in pain often. She rushes to the bathroom often. She has blood at the back of her dress often. She smells an awful putrid rotting smell all about her like it's oozing from the pores of her skin. And she screams, "You don't know what pain is. Just you wait. You'll see." And she slams the door on me.

A door, a rope, a death. The message is clear. I am cut off and floating in a space all my own without even a cloud to look at, with no warm arms to embrace me and pull me down. And I don't want to grow up. I don't want to move. I don't even want to leave the bathroom.

I cradle a bottle of salve my daddy made, long ago, maybe even before I was born. I found it tucked way back in one of the cabinet shelves by the Vaseline and cotton balls. I unscrew the black lid and smell the familiar lanolin smell. The daddy who could do anything, even invent salves that could heal sore muscles and traumatized skin. His special formula, made one day in Gramma's basement. It might have been just the thing to make him a millionaire. He was certain something would. But the salve is getting old. Those little jars—every aunt and uncle and grandparent and cousin and second cousin twice removed has one tucked away somewhere. I rub the smooth cool bottle. I look at the stain in the bathtub. I look at myself in the mirror. I hate the sad girl who looks back at me.

Then the familiar knock. The knock at the door. Mary Ruth needs to come in. I have to get it together. This Christmas morning feels no different than all the school mornings that blur together in my mind. Each day I go to my room, put on some putrid, so-bad-they-never-were-in-style-anyway clothes, pick up my books and papers from somewhere in the mess of things crumpled and scattered on the floor, and then walk to school. Then I sit there to absorb information class to class to class all day.

But nothing I learn in school sticks for long. Once a test is over, it's gone, like I never learned a thing. And when I feel shaky like this, nothing sticks at all. And I feel this shaky thing more and more often. That red brown ring around the bathtub sticks though. I take the Ajax from under the sink, and the rag, full of holes, recycled from dishwashing duty. I run tap water over the rag and squeeze, and then I pour the cleanser all around the ring. I scrub, and I scrub. Mary Ruth knocks louder.

"I'll be right out, I say." But I keep scrubbing, scrubbing. I pour more cleanser and scrub more.

Mary Ruth bangs louder; "Hurry up," she says. "I have to go.

"So do I," Kathy calls out. "

Then Mommy's voice thunders through, "What's the matter, Laura, did you fall in?" And she laughs. Again she laughs, a bitter taunting laugh at a twisted joke nobody else has ever found amusing. I turn the water on full blast, and rinse away the grainy cleanser suds. The stain remains, exactly as it was.

Mary Ruth knocks again. "Please, Laura. Hurry up."

I put the cleanser and rag back under the sink, turn the doorknob, and I walk out to the hallway, brushing up against her. Mary Ruth got her first period months ago. Kathy, the eldest, and I, the youngest, could get ours any day. I suppose Kathy will get hers before I get mine since she's two years older. Does Mary Ruth see the ring? Does Kathy? Of course they do. How could they miss it? But do we talk about it? No.

Maybe Mommy isn't fixing the stain on purpose. Maybe it isn't that she can't find some way to get rid of it. Maybe she won't. Maybe she needs it to remind us of how bad things are. As if we need reminding. We know we aren't the only ones wounded. Even the house is wounded. Look. The stain is proof. The house is crying and bleeding and creaking and smudging too, and I want to fall on my knees and crawl and beg someone, anyone, to please, please help us, but I don't know who to call or what to say. But it doesn't matter because as soon as I step into the hallway, the urge to lose control and plead for help goes away. And I'm glad, relieved to assume my happy-go-lucky, quick-thinking, oh-it's-a-new-kind-of-shampoo, tried-and-true persona. "Oh, it's a new kind of shampoo" is what I said when I came to school with clean hair, a rare occurrence because Mommy lets us wash our hair only once a month so as not to waste water. This girl Zara, who knows everything about fashion and already wears shiny pink lipstick and black eyeliner in perfect strokes both above and below her eyes, came up to my lunch table. She tugged my hair and said, "Your hair looks so nice and shiny today, Laura. What did you do?"

I couldn't tell her the truth. I couldn't tell her all I'd done was wash it. I told her I'd used a new shampoo.

She said, "What kind?"

I wasn't off the hook yet, I had to keep thinking. "I don't know, but it was real thick and green," I said.

"Oh, it must be Prell Concentrate. I've seen it advertised on TV," she offered.

"Yeah, that's it. Prell Concentrate," I lied, knowing name-brand shampoos never grace our bathroom shelves.

Then she went on her way to return her lunch tray to the cafeteria staff since she was one of those kids who actually buys a hot lunch at school, unlike me. I bring peanut butter and marshmallow fluff sandwiches just about every day. I hate this.

I must make something else real besides this life. I cannot stand this wringing, clinging sadness everywhere inside me, surrounding me, throughout me in every breath, and it deepens day by day. I am entrenched and lost, and Mommy in her own private hell has other things on her mind. If I cross her mind at all, it's not concern for me or love or anything like that she feels. It's resentment that I am young and physically healthy and someday I'll be able to leave her, but where will I go? Who will want me?

Why is everything falling apart like this—like pieces of us crashing down to the ground as we ride on a train speeding out of control to a destination. But where? Why won't it stop? Why can't it stop even for just a day or two so I can just sit still with my arms around my knees and look at ants crawling in the dirt, so I can tell the world how angry I am, so I can stand up and say that you can't speed me on like this. You have to give me my daddy back, or give me something, even a scrapbook to hug close to my heart and tuck under my pillow, something other than this on and on, this screaming in the house and me marching in step through the seasons, the snow, the rain, the beautiful sunshine. March, march, march, sick or well. Pause to vomit if you really must, but pick yourself up and get to school to sit in a desk and listen and write and regurgitate and march back home to hope the door isn't locked, to hope Mommy isn't mad, but to know she will be, to sit at the table and pound holes in the top with the tip of your pen through the tablecloth because she is screaming and you can't think, and the TV's blaring and the phone is ringing, and the radio's going, and you are ashamed because the table, the sleek Danish Modern table, was the last piece of furniture Daddy bought in the last year he was alive, actually it was the only piece of furniture you ever saw him buy, and now you've ruined it. It can't be fixed. Nothing can be fixed, and there is no escape.

Mary Ruth bursts into the bathroom after me like water flowing through a hole in a dam. We all have to get ready for church. It's Christmas, after all. We've been going to church almost every week since Daddy died. One of Daddy's last wishes was that Kathy, Mary Ruth and I return to the church. When Mommy first brought it up right after Daddy's funeral she said "the Church," not "a church" or just "church." We all knew that meant our Church, the Catholic Church. The Catholic church closest to us, the only Catholic church in Hinsdale, is St. Isaac Jogues.

This news was a relief to me. It meant I could stop living a sort of double life. Daddy was angry with the Church for as far back as I can remember, but not completely angry. He turned away, but not so far that he wouldn't set foot inside a chapel, not so far that he would ever forget to bow his head, cross himself and say grace before each meal, not so far that he ever ate meat on Friday, and not so far that he let any relatives other than Gramma and Unc know that we weren't going to mass regularly and that he wasn't sending us to those Saturday classes that are held especially for Catholic kids who attend public school.

Mommy says Daddy's break with the Church had to do with a priest who insulted him in a private conversation around the time Mary Agnes died. That's why Daddy and Mommy got married at a Justice of the Peace instead of in a church. "It's not like we couldn't get married in a church," she insisted when I asked about it. "Oh, I suppose you think it's because I've got the heebie jeebies, and don't deny it. I know you. I know what you think, but you're wrong. I was raised Catholic too, you know, but your father didn't want to have anything to do with a church wedding. That priest did it to him."

I have tried at different times to get Mommy to say what the priest said to get Daddy so mad, but she says, "Only God knows that, smarty pants. Maybe they're talking in Heaven right now. I don't know. Keep your big nose to yourself."

At Daddy's funeral lots of people stared at us when Kathy, Mary Ruth and I sat huddled in our pew instead of lining up so that Father Walsh could stick a wafer on our tongues at communion time. At eleven, twelve and thirteen years of age we were well past when we should have had our first holy communions. Everybody knew that. We had managed to fake it during his wake. Each priest who came into the funeral parlor room—ours for two days and three nights—set my heart to beating real fast at some point during his visit. All eyes would be on him as he made his way up to the coffin, shaking hands with people he knew along the way. Then he'd say a silent prayer or two on his knees at the coffin. Then before he'd greet Mommy, who was always either sitting or standing by the head of the coffin, the priest would turn around to face the crowd of mourners and call us all to prayer.

Since Kathy, Mary Ruth and I were the daughters of the deceased, we had to go up front near the coffin and get on our knees on the rough mauve-colored rug. As we knelt people stuffed rosaries in our hands. We fumbled with them, knowing nothing about what beads go with what prayers, and pretended like it was all old hat. All the while I'd be looking over at Daddy's cropped hair sticking up against the lining of his coffin. His hair, in life, was always combed back off his forehead, but then as the day wore on it would loosen a little and start dipping down over his brow a bit. It irked me that not only had they chopped him up inside, they'd made his hair look like someone had run a lawn mower over it. Daddy's hair and trying to look sure of myself as I held the rosary beads were what occupied my mind as I mumbled through hundreds of Our Fathers and Hail Marys. I could probably say them backwards if I had to now. But at the funeral, there's no way Kathy, Mary Ruth and I could fake taking communion from our seats. And we couldn't march up there with everybody else because God would probably strike us dead if we took communion before we had been properly prepared. So we were exposed as the really bad Catholics that we are.

When I turned seven, Grampa O'Neill came to give me a jar of pennies—like he did for each of his grandchildren every year—and to take Kathy, Mary Ruth and me out for lunch with Uncle Dean. Before we left for lunch Grampa looked at the three of us and smiled and said, "My, my, look at how fast you're all growing." And then he asked Mommy, "Isn't it about time the girls had their first holy communions?"

I thought we were really busted at that point, but before anybody could say anything, Mommy said, "Oh, they already had their communions, right here at St. Isaac's." She flat out lied, something she says we're never supposed to do.

Grampa looked shocked, almost like she'd just thrown a cup of coffee on him. His face flushed red and he sucked in his breath. I think he felt really bad that he hadn't been invited. I wanted to tell him, "Grampa, I'd go have my first holy communion if I could, and you'd be one of the first people I'd invite." But I knew saying that to Grampa would get me in all sorts of trouble.

Four years later, I couldn't get Mommy's lie out of my mind at Daddy's funeral. It lingered inside me just like the smell of incense still hung in the air from when Father Walsh shook this little silver ball on a chain with pungent smoke pouring out of it. He'd said some beautiful Latin phrases as his wrist flicked the ball out and back, out and back, over Daddy's coffin. I wondered as I breathed the scent deep into my nostrils how my grampa was feeling, knowing we were unable to take communion at our own father's service. I was eager to put an end to all this weird secrecy. The first Sunday right after Daddy's funeral when we drove in Mommy's Chevy to mass at St. Isaac's, I had absolutely no objection.

I can't say that I really liked being there at St. Isaac Jogues. Going to mass was always so much work, so much up and down and being on edge trying to figure out what's coming next and being prepared. Then there was Father Walsh. He had a reputation for having a mean temper. His reputation penetrated far beyond the Catholic community into homes all around Hinsdale. Kids tried hard not to get on his bad side. But it was so easy to do. We heard the kids who went to school at St. Isaac's lived in terror that he might come into one of their classrooms and drag them out of class for some punishment. Sometimes I thought I'd rather meet the headless horseman from *The Legend of Sleepy Hollow* than sit face to face with Father Walsh. Returning to the Church meant we were going to have to do just that. Face Father Walsh. I was sure we already had two strikes against us for all the masses and instruction we'd missed. I didn't know if we could ever make it up, but I wanted to try.

Mommy told Father Walsh after that first mass we went to after Daddy's funeral that she would call him to arrange for us to start instruction. Several weeks went by. We'd managed to avoid Father Walsh after Sunday mass, but on the next Sunday, Father Walsh was scowling at all of us when we tried to slip by him after the service. We were right at the curb, about to cross the street to the parking lot when he caught up to us. He steered Mommy aside, away from the three of us. I couldn't hear what either of them was saying, but his face was getting red, and he was gesturing at her wildly with his hands. She was standing there, looking very small and meek. For an adult Mommy is really small, just under 5 feet tall. Kathy and Mary Ruth have been taller than Mommy for ages, and now I finally am too. Father Walsh isn't as tall as Daddy was—Daddy was 5 feet 11 inches, almost a whole 6 feet tall. But still, compared to Father Walsh, Mommy looked tiny. In fact she seemed to shrink as Father Walsh spoke to her. It was cold outside, so all around her face, I could see the steam from his breath pressing in.

Finally, I guess he'd said enough. He turned away from Mommy and walked up to another of his parishioners. With her mouth closed real tight, Mommy walked over to us, exaggerating her limp. Then she said, "Come on, girls, let's get out of this stinkin' place."

We piled into the car, Kathy in front with Mommy, Mary Ruth and me in the back. Mommy started up the engine and then very slowly backed out of her parking space, turned the wheel, got the car in drive and inched out of the lot. Mommy is a really bad driver, especially when it comes to getting in and out of parking spaces, and especially if those spaces are parallel parking spots. We sometimes sit in the car with her for fifteen minutes or more while she huffs and groans, pulling the steering wheel hard in one direction and then another, and inching the car up and back a teeny bit at a time, working her way in or out of a space. I was thankful that at least there was no parallel parking in the St. Isaac's lot, which, I think, doubles as a playground during the week. But it still took her a long time to ease away. I had my fingers crossed, hoping that nobody was staring at us. I'm sure we must have looked like we were in a slow-motion movie.

Once Mommy got the car out on the street and she didn't have to concentrate as much, she started muttering. I could tell right away she was working herself into one of her talking fits. I was hoping it wasn't going to be one where she asks us questions, answers for us before we have a chance to get a word out of our mouths, and then gets angry at us for the answers she makes up for us. When she's having one of these weird episodes, even if we do manage to get a thought of our own out there, she twists it into something we didn't say. Kathy, Mary Ruth and I just kept real quiet, listening. A lot of things she says are things I've heard countless times before, but every so often she throws in a little zinger, something nobody has ever said before, like a little something that may or may not be a piece of the puzzle of my life, depending upon whether it's true or not.

"Who does he think he is, that Father Walsh? God? Yeah, he thinks he's God himself walking on earth, he does. That miserable piece of, oh Hell's bells, what do I give a damn about what he thinks, telling me what I should and shouldn't do? Big as you please, just like God. What right does he have? Him and that damn, cold church. Why should we even bother going there, being treated like that? What does he know of my obligations, obligations to your parents, girls, your parents, your dead parents, I might add, what does he think I am, a piece of shit? Yeah, that's it, probably just a worthless piece of cow dung who owes something to your dead parents. What do they care, especially your mother? If she matters so much, she can just crawl out of her grave and take care of you herself. But she wouldn't want to do that. Did you know you three locked her out of the house one time? Oh, yes indeed, little demons, your father told me all about it. He told me to look out for you. Yes he did. He warned me to watch out. He found her there, the end of the day, on the front porch crying while you were inside tearing the house apart. You girls had locked your mother, your very own mother out, and you wouldn't let her back inside. You devils incarnate, you didn't even have any love and compassion for your own mother. You, and Father Walsh, and your damn mother. What do I owe anybody? I'm your mother. I'm the one in charge here. He can take his whole church and shove it up my ass. That's what he can do with it. And if he doesn't like it, he can lump it. He can. God and everybody else can just lump it too. Yeah. Telling me I'm a bad parent, a bad parent because I haven't enrolled you in classes yet. How dare he. What does he know about what bad children you are? I'll show him."

She kept that up throughout our four-block drive home. The thing that was new was the story about Kathy, Mary Ruth and me locking Mary Agnes out of the house. After Mommy pulled the car into the drive, we got out quick and rushed out of the car. When we were coming through the front door I asked Mary Ruth, "Do you think we really did that, locked our mother out of the house?"

"Maybe. I don't remember."

As we hung up our coats in the hall closet, I asked Kathy, "Do you remember locking our mother outside of our house?"

"I don't remember much of anything about what we did with her. But, you know, I think if we did that, it was an accident, you know, just one of those things that happens."

Mary Ruth added, "And you know, maybe she even locked herself out by mistake and now, you know the way Mommy is, it's like that telephone game where what one person says at one end of a line of people gets completely changed by the time it reaches the person at the other end. Only with Mommy, she's the whole line, and everything gets twisted inside her own head."

We all laughed at that. Mommy had just come inside. She looked at us suspiciously and asked, "What are you three demons laughing at?"

"That game Telephone, where people pass a sentence from one person to another and it gets all twisted by the time it reaches the last person," Kathy said.

"Oh, well I suppose you have better things to do, like homework, than to laugh about some party game right now," Mommy said.

Later that afternoon, she called us into the dining room.

When we were all seated at the table she said, "Girls, I know you've been asking to have more voice in decisions. Kathy's been asking for family meetings where we talk about things. Well, we're going to have a family meeting right now about this whole church business."

Mommy was being really nice. She was giving us the part of her that could be normal, and sweet, and even funny enough to make us all laugh. It's true we had been asking to have family meetings ever since she told us we had to give Muffin away. It was too late to talk about Muffin; he was already gone, but we wanted to talk about a lot of other things. Way high up on the list was what we call her. All the other kids, boys and girls, have been calling their parents Mom and Dad for quite some time, some even started in fifth grade. But Mommy's been dead set against us calling her Mom. We can't figure out why. We thought if we all talked about it, she might see our point of view, how other kids think it's really babyish to call your mom Mommy.

Another thing we wanted to talk about was us having to be home from school every day at 5 p.m. That's when Mommy locks the front door and puts supper out on the counter for us. Most of the time, we don't need to be out that long. Even when there's an activity like chorus or the school paper, things usually wrap up by 4:00 p.m. It's easy to get home by 4:30. But sometimes on Fridays at the junior high school, where I still go to school, there are basketball games. Lots of kids go to them. There are parties too. And for Kathy and Mary Ruth there are all kinds of activities at the high school. We've never been able to go to any of them if they last past 4:30 p.m. Mommy has never let us go to a single game or party. Period.

I was thinking having this family meeting about church was maybe the start of us really having a voice in what goes on. I was feeling optimistic, even though it was about something that wasn't on the list of important family matters Kathy, Mary Ruth and I kept in our minds.

So there, with the pelican in our mural looking on, Mommy said, "I've been thinking a lot about St. Isaac Jogues. It's not a very friendly church now is it? I've never really been comfortable there, have you?"

Each of us answered honestly, "No."

"So I was thinking we should visit some other churches first before we officially become members of St. Isaac's, shop around a little. There's St. Joseph's in Downers Grove where Uncle Jack and Aunt Dorothy go. We could go there. It's a much nicer place. Would you like that?"

"Yeah, sure," Mary Ruth said.

"Isn't that a little far away, I mean, it would be a longer drive, and if we went to classes on Saturdays, how would we get there? You'd have to drive us there too. We can walk to St. Isaac's," Kathy said.

I just kept quiet, mulling this over.

"Maybe it would be better to try a different church here in Hinsdale," Mommy said.

"St. Isaac's is the only Catholic church in town," I said.

"Yes, Laura, that's true," Mommy replied. "But I think just about any church, if it was a real Christian church would be true to your father's wishes."

"But we're Catholic." Mary Ruth said.

"Oh, we have been, but pretty much in name only. I don't think your father could have been thinking straight then, just before he died. Come on now, could you think straight with all those nuns and priests hovering over you for six weeks straight, working on you to come back to God. Of course, he did put his wish into words, and I promised him I'd get you girls going to church. I thought we could visit the Lutheran church next week. It's not far from here. Any other ideas?"

"There's Union Church right by the junior high school," Kathy suggested.

"Yeah, I'd like to see what that church is like. Lots of kids from school go there," I said.

"We'll go there the week after, and we'll keep looking until we've found the right place."

"And it might be St. Isaac Jogues," I said.

"Possibly," Mommy said, smiling at the three of us. "Now I think this family meeting has gone very well. We'll have another one after we've done some church visiting."

"We have some other things to talk about," Kathy said.

"If you give 'em an inch, they take a mile. That's so true of you girls. What do you mean you have other things to talk about? Who do you think you are?"

"Well, there's whether we can call you Mom instead of Mommy. That's one thing," Kathy said.

"Oh, for Christ's sake. You can't leave well enough alone, can you."

"What's wrong with calling you Mom?" Mary Ruth added.

"You girls are always pressing for more, more, more. Well listen, things are different now. If you want to complain, do it somewhere else. If you're all of a sudden so grown up you can't even call me Mommy, why don't you find another place to live? Go on, if you're so smart, the three of you, you ought to be able to make it on your own. I'm through with this rigamarole."

"Oh, forget it," Kathy said. She got up, slamming the palms of her hands down hard on the table, pushed off, and ran down the hall.

"Yeah," Mary Ruth said getting up too, "And I don't care what stupid church we go to, okay? Does it really matter what we think anyway?"

"Mary Ruth, come back here this instant," Mommy ordered. But Mary Ruth had already left the room, following Kathy down the hall.

Mommy got up from the table and limped into the kitchen, scratching her elbows as she walked. I sat at the table looking out the dining room window at big snow drifts piled along the curb from where snow ploughs had cleared the road. I wondered if I could dig into one of those mounds and make myself an igloo. It had never worked before, but I got up, put on my coat, hat, boots, gloves, scarf, went outside, pulled a rusty trowel out of the garage, and started to dig.

I didn't really know what to think of this visiting other churches idea. We did try the Lutheran church first, which just seemed dull and drab and somber with none of the Catholic church's mysteriousness. Then we went to the church Kathy suggested across from the junior high school playground. It's called the Union Church of Hinsdale because it was created a long time ago when a Unitarian church and a Congregationalist church combined to form one church.

There are lots of things I like about Union Church. First there are genuinely friendly people who talk to us in

the vestibule before and after the services, second there's
no kneeling, third there's no Latin to learn, fourth nobody
gets angry if you miss a week's service, fifth, lots of kids
from school go there, sixth everybody can take communion
from tiny vials they pass around in a big round tray, and
best of all is the music. People sing hymns before, after and
between every part of the service. Everybody sings out loud
and strong. It's a powerful feeling when the church is filled
with all those voices blending in harmony. So it's easy to like
Union Church.

We went to Union Church several weeks in a row. Then
Mommy asked, "Well girls, what do you think? Do you want
to join Union Church?"

I don't know what Kathy and Mary Ruth were thinking,
but I knew that's what Mommy wanted to do, just by the way
she had been saying all these nice things about the church
and all these bad things about St. Isaac's. Kathy and Mary
Ruth said okay to joining Union Church. So did I. I knew it
was going to happen anyway.

A few weeks passed by, and then along came Father
Walsh, ringing our doorbell. I answered the door.

"Hello, Laura."

"Hello, Father."

"Is your mother home? I'd like to speak with her."

"Yes, of course." I let him in. I hoped he couldn't see that
I was trembling as I took his fuzzy black hat and thick black
wool coat. I put them over a chair near the door and gestured
for him to sit down in the dining room.

"Hello, Father," Mommy called from the kitchen. "Would
you like a cup of coffee?"

"Yes," he replied. She was already in the room, carrying the coffee pot and an empty cup. As she poured, he asked, "Why haven't I heard from you? What's wrong? You know you're falling down on your duty to these girls, not to mention yourself as well, but especially these innocent girls."

"Oh, Father, I don't think you need to worry."

"Not worry? How can I not worry about all of your souls?" Then he spoke at length about how we needed to be going to religious instruction on Saturday mornings and how we were already way behind where we should be. He mentioned that Mommy was a disappointment to him.

Finally Mommy interrupted him saying, "Well Father, actually, the girls won't be going to you for religions instruction."

"Why is that? St. Isaac's is the closest parish. Certainly it makes sense to be close to home."

"Oh, yes, Father, it does. They'll be close to home. Just not in your church."

"What do you mean?" he said putting down his coffee cup and glaring at Mommy.

"Well, we've decided to join Union Church, so we'll be going there instead."

"Union Church? These are Catholic girls. You have an obligation to their parents and to God to raise them Catholic." His voice was rising higher and higher.

Mommy responded, "Well, I don't see it that way."

He stood up and screamed, "Who are you to question God's authority?"

"I am their mother," Mommy screamed back, "and I have the authority to do exactly what I want."

He walked to the chair where I'd put his hat and coat. As he put them on he looked at me and said, "God have mercy on your soul, my child." Then he looked at Mommy, pointing his finger at her like a gun and said, "You're going to burn in Hell for this!"

His voice filled the room like a car backfiring right by my ear. I expected at that point that a lightning bolt would strike our home and split it in half right where Mommy stood. But nothing happened. We all trembled in the silence that followed. Then Father Walsh turned, opened the door slamming it hard into the brass cylindrical wind chimes Mommy had just hung in the hall. Then he kicked the storm door open with his shiny black boot, and walked outside. The storm door slapped closed behind him. I tiptoed up under the clanging wind chime, watched him stomp away, and then gently, slowly closed the door.

I returned to the dining room table and Mommy said, "I'm certainly going to be relieved not to see him anymore."

I didn't feel that way. Union Church for me is mostly a social thing, and a chance to be filled with beautiful music. But as far as God and meaning and where I belong, I fear it's really at St. Isaac Jogues. Each week I feel I'm taking a step farther away from myself and from what my father really wanted by basking in the music that fills the Union Church sanctuary. But I don't think it's as awful as what Father Walsh said. I don't think Mommy's going to burn in Hell. And sometimes I think what does it matter anyway? I've heard there are all these changes coming to the Catholic Church from this big meeting called Vatican Two. Some people say it means that Catholics will be more like Protestants in lots of ways. I just wish I could know for sure what Daddy thought about all of this, since our returning to the church was his last wish and really ought to be respected.

Unc goes to mass every week. I wonder what he thinks about Union Church, but I can't bring myself to ask him. He still comes to visit just about every Saturday. I love seeing his blue Buick sedan pull into our driveway. One time he bought us a lifeline in the form of three black transistor radios. They're so small you can hold one in the palm of your hand. Since he teaches math at a junior high school, he knows that just about every kid listens to Dick Biondi on WLS radio. He also knows that just about every kid goes to dances, has friends over after school, goes to slumber parties, and movies on Saturdays too. The radios for us are part of his helping us have more of a normal life.

He pushes Mommy in gentle ways, asking questions, posing ideas, but never getting her dander up so that her temper flares. In fact, for a time, I think Mommy was a little sweet on him. That's part of why he could ask her things without her getting mad at him.

She asked me one day, "What would you think if I married your Uncle John?"

"I dunno," I said, all the while thinking that putting the two of them together just seemed weird.

"What about Elmer? He asked me, you know, to be his wife. Maybe I should have said yes," she said.

"Elmer?" I couldn't picture him being part of our family. He was our Jewel Tea salesman. If Fred Flintstone dressed in a brown uniform and had black horn-rimmed glasses with super-thick lenses, he'd look like Elmer's twin. Elmer came around more often than most traveling salesmen. The Cook Coffee man just came once a month or so, but Elmer came by about once a week. It was always a treat when he opened up his case and gave us a big show of gadgets and gizmos, whirligigs, and fancy foods. Mommy always bought something small, like maybe a plastic fold up rain hat, or a box of crackers. I was surprised when he showed up with presents for all of us on Christmas Eve last year. That was 1961, my second Christmas without Daddy. For Mommy he brought a big bottle of Channel No. 5 perfume and a necklace of real pearls, not cultured ones. For each of us he brought a sterling silver necklace with two little heart charms on it.

"What's the matter?" Mommy asked, "Cat got your tongue? Do you think I'm too unattractive for any man to want me? Whose fault do you think that is? That wild dog Muffin is it. He's the cause. I have this big scar down my nose thanks to him."

Mommy was talking about the day she drove in a car with Muffin in the front seat. He slid off the seat, leaned over the hump in the middle of the floor, and started barfing on her right foot, the one on the gas pedal. She reached down to push him away, lost control of the car, and smacked into a tree. The car just had some minor damage to the bumper, but Mommy's nose got a gash from the bridge to maybe half way down to her nostrils on the right side.

"I never notice the scar, Mommy. I don't think other people do either," I said, lying.

"So you think I was unattractive even before the accident."

"If Daddy liked you, then I think lots of other men would probably like you too," I said, "but it would be hard to imagine anybody but Daddy being with us."

"Oh, don't worry. I know there aren't many men alive who could hold a candle to your dad. Not in my eyes. I'm in no rush to get married again," she said.

I was glad to hear that. I didn't want Elmer for a father, and I was worried that if Unc married Mommy he'd really be hers, not Kathy's, Mary Ruth's and mine, like he is now.

Unc is the closest thing to a dad we have, coming over like he does. Kathy told him about Mommy not letting us have friends over. He asked Mommy, in private so as not to embarrass her, what her reasons were for keeping our friends out of the house. She said there just wasn't enough room in the house for our friends. Some people fix up their basements and turn a part of them in recreation rooms, but our basement leaks in water every time it rains more than a little sprinkle. If we get a big thunderstorm, it floods. I remember up until I was in second grade or so Daddy kept having contractors come in to try to fix it. Finally, he gave up, bought a dehumidifier, and we just live with this big flaw, a basement that is always damp and sometimes full of two to three inches of water with papers and balloons and all manner of other things we've forgotten were on the floor swirling around in the muck. So fixing up the basement for us was out of the question. But Unc took care of the problem. He added a little room just for us; it's right off the living room. He hired other people to do the foundation and framing, and he worked on weekends with our cousin George to finish it. They put our little room together lickety split.

He also made Kathy, Mary Ruth and me a combination radio/stereo console. It is such a fine solid piece of furniture. We were completely surprised when he brought it in the door. The biggest thing I'd dared to ever dream about was a portable record player like a lot of girls have. Our stereo must be six feet long with big built-in speakers for glorious sound. I am so amazed by its beauty and the fact that Unc made it by hand, sometimes I just get mesmerized looking at it, touching it, before I even turn it on.

Mommy says we can forget about inviting friends over to use the room, that bringing in outsiders was never part of the plan; having the stereo should be enough for us, and if we don't pipe down she'll tell Unc just how ungrateful we are for all he's done. So she uses the room a couple times a month for a card club of her Aunt Dorothy's that she joined. I don't know why she hangs out with a bunch of women who are all at least twenty years older than she is. They all live near Aunt Dorothy too; Mommy doesn't have any friends in Hinsdale. But even though Mommy's the only one who gets to have friends over, Kathy, Mary Ruth and I still get to spend time in the room listening to 45s we buy with our baby-sitting money.

We practice dances—the twist, jitterbug, things like that—for someday when we get to go to dances. I bought Bobby Darrin's song *Multiplication* last year, and this year I bought *Sherry* by the Four Seasons. I love dancing to our records. We also brought up stacks of old 45s from the basement that Mommy got a long time ago when she worked at WIND radio. They're tunes that never got played much and never went anywhere on the charts. But there are a few we like to dance to. Mary Ruth and I practice jitterbugging—toe-heel, toe-heel, back, step—to a record called *Beatnik Fly*. We're really bad at the jitterbug. I guess you'd say we're real clods.

A lot of kids watch *American Bandstand* in the afternoon and practice dancing to that, but we only have the TV on at night, and only to programs Mommy wants to watch— *Bonanza, Sea Hunt, Gun Smoke, Lawrence Welk*—things like that. Even though I didn't pick them, I still look forward to them each week. I'm especially attached to Little Joe on *Bonanza*. I think Adam is pretty cool too.

In sixth grade, a lot of kids signed up for something called Fortnightly. They learned old-fashioned dances like the cha cha and the fox trot, but they also learned the jitterbug and all sorts of variations on the twist. One day in the summer before I started sixth grade, when I was fetching Daddy's golf balls in the backyard, I asked him if I could go to Fortnightly. This, I knew, was out of line because Kathy and Mary Ruth hadn't been able to go. The notices came in the mail first for Kathy and then the next year for Mary Ruth. Mommy just threw them away. No discussion. I knew I shouldn't ask for something they hadn't been able to do, but I really wanted to learn to dance. So I asked, "Daddy, may I go to Fortnightly in the fall?"

It's the only thing I can remember ever asking him for. Something just for me. He paused there, leaning on his golf club, just looking into the clouds. Then very seriously he said, "Yes, Laura. You can go to Fortnightly."

I was on cloud nine for the rest of the summer thinking about being able to be part of that dancing group. But when the Fortnightly notice came for me, Daddy was in the hospital, and Fortnightly just became like one of the fish at the feet of the pelican on our mural, very dead. But now with Unc making that room and building us a stereo too, I'm finding another way to learn to dance.

Unc sends us to the movies sometimes on Saturdays too. He'll hand Kathy enough money to get us inside and buy soda and candy too, and tell us to just take off. We'll usually be in the middle of something like pulling dandelions and crabgrass out of the lawn by the roots with these long skinny fork-like weed-pulling things. It takes hours to scour the lawn, even with all three of us working. Plus dandelions and crab grass are always growing back. It's one of those jobs that never ends. Mommy loves those. Then, if she runs out of ideas for things that really need to be done, she has us move the living room furniture around. After maybe an hour or so, it ends up right back where it started. Sometimes we even just move boxes around on the planks that serve as a floor in the attic.

The first time Unc sent us to the movies we just stood there for a while looking at the heap of quarters and nickels Unc had put in Kathy's hand. Mommy only likes us going to movies when she decides it's a good idea, and it's always at the theater in Downers Grove. I'd only been to the Hinsdale Theater once in my life before. That was to see *Bambi*. We went as a family all together when Daddy was alive. I cried silently, tears just running down my face when Bambi's mother died. I looked on each side of me, and Kathy and Mary Ruth were crying too. Now Unc was sending us to Hinsdale Theater on our own.

We were afraid to put down our weed pullers and just walk off to the movie.

"What about Mommy?" Kathy asked.

Unc replied, "Don't worry, girls. Go have a good time. I'll be here when you get back."

It was hard not to worry, but I didn't think Unc would ever tell us something he didn't mean. So we set off and watched *The Blob* and got ourselves so scared that now we imagine that red gooey slippery shiny sludge stuff coming through the heat vents in our house. First it's just a drop or two, then a trickle, then it comes pouring through all the vents so fast that the vents finally break off the wall, and the Blob floods in and slurps each of us up. That's what we think is about to happen any minute. But still, it was worth it, going off on our own to see a movie in town on a Saturday. I saw lots of kids from school there. I don't know what Unc said to Mommy, but she didn't complain one little bit when we got home, not even after he left. Her resentment of our choice in music comes out loud and strong though.

Sometimes we turn on our stereo so we can play our records, and nothing happens. The first time we ran to Mommy and asked her what to do. She said, "Oh, there's nothing you can do. If it won't turn on, I guess it's broken."

We didn't want to give up that fast. We couldn't believe Unc would make something that would break, especially since it had worked fine just the day before. We all poked around, and Kathy happened to look behind the stereo and see that it was unplugged from the wall socket. She plugged it in, and it was just fine. Mommy didn't seem at all happy that we'd gotten it working again. About a week later, we came home from school and found that some of our records had been scratched. Kathy asked Mommy, "Do you know what happened to our records?"

"What do you mean?" Mommy asked.

Kathy held the scratched 45s in front of Mommy's nose.

"Look," she said.

"I don't know what happened."

"Somebody must have scratched them," Kathy said.

"You probably did it yourself," Mommy accused.

"No, we didn't scratch our own records. They were fine yesterday," Kathy said.

"Then some strangers must have come into the house when I was out in the backyard earlier. That's all I can think of. That means I'll have to start locking the door even when I'm home," Mommy said.

"Strangers? What strangers?" Kathy asked.

"I don't know. I saw some suspicious looking people standing across the street this morning."

"Suspicious looking people? What did they look like?" Kathy probed.

"Oh, for Christ's sakes. I don't have to explain anything to you. Now leave me be. You probably scratched the records yourself. You know how careless you all are. Honestly getting so worked up about a few records. You do carry on, Katherine."

We were sure Mommy had unplugged the stereo and scratched our records, but we had no proof. Then we found out she was messing with our transistor radios too. We like to put them under our pillows and listen to WLS long after bedtime. I loved especially hearing Shelly Fabares singing *Johnny Angel* when I was falling asleep last year. That's when that song was really popular. Her voice is so smooth, like ice cream, only not cold. Songs like that make me think about the boys at school. I don't have a crush on anybody, and nobody has a crush on me. But I wonder what it would be like. Some kids started having real boyfriend/girlfriend relationships back in sixth grade. I can't imagine how to go about something like that, but I hope someday I'll have a Johnny Angel of my own to love.

When Kathy, Mary Ruth and I go to school, we leave our radios under our pillows. It wasn't too long after our records got scratched up that Mary Ruth and I both noticed that our radios were on real low when we got home from school. I thought maybe we forgot to turn them off, but Mary Ruth thought it was odd that both of us would forget on the same day. We checked with Kathy, and she'd found her radio on too. We decided the next morning to check all of our radios to make sure they were off before we left for school. When we got home, each of us found our radios turned on.

We found Mommy in her reclining chair. She sat on the couch when Daddy was alive, but now his old recliner is hers. It's getting so I can't even picture him in it anymore. We stood in the hallway right near her chair, and perilously close to one of our heat vents. We held our transistor radios in our open palms, slightly away from our bodies, as though we were each carrying a crown on a pillow or something. Mommy looked up from her *Family Circle* magazine and said, "All right, what do you want now?"

"It's about our radios. We've been finding them turned on when we get home from school," Kathy said.

"I don't know a thing bout your damn radios, girls," she said.

"Yes, you do," Kathy said, "You've been turning them on during the day to use up our batteries."

"Yeah, you know we don't have the money to keep

replacing the batteries," Mary Ruth added.

"Don't be ridiculous, girls," she sneered, "If your radios are on, you did it yourselves. Don't blame me."

"We know you did it," Kathy said.

"Are you calling me a liar?"

"Yes," Kathy said, "Yes, we are. All three of us are."

"Oh, I doubt that, Katherine. You probably put your sisters up to this. You're always trying to manipulate them so you can be in charge of everything here. I know you and your ways. Mary Ruth, you're not calling me a liar, are you?"

"Yes, yes I am," she said.

"Oh, I should have known you would, big fat smarty pants, you great big know-it-all. You more than anybody, looking down your big fat honker at me. Well, surely Laura, you won't turn against me, the only mother who stuck around to wipe your smelly behind when you were little, you won't turn against me. I know I can count on you, can't I?"

I really didn't want things to be going the way they were, to have to make this choice, to declare myself, to either be with her and against my sisters and me, or against her and for my sisters and me. I thought about some of the nice things she's done. Like in sixth grade, out of the blue in early March she asked me if I wanted to have a St. Patrick's Day party. I said yes. She got little shamrock favors, and green paper plates, muffins with green frosting, green napkins, green chocolate mints. I invited six girls from class, and they all came on a Saturday afternoon. It was a good day for Mommy too. She sat at the table with us, and said sweet things to everybody, even me, calling me honey and peanut and sweetie. When I was saying good-bye to Tricia, who has probably the most beautiful mommy in the world—long wavy blond hair like a shampoo model and clothes that look like they're straight from a commercial for Ivory soap—Tricia leaned close to me and said, "Laura, your mother is nice." And it's true, on that day she was. But most of the time, it's like walking across the desert with everything nice about her in some oasis, always far-off on the horizon.

I also thought about the time Kathy and Mary Ruth fought with Mommy for permission to shave their legs. They argued and argued. That was when I was in sixth grade too and nobody in my class was shaving her legs yet. But just about all of the seventh and eighth grade girls were doing it. Finally, Mommy said, "Oh, go ahead. Be like those slutty movie stars—Marilyn Monroe, Elizabeth Taylor. You know Taylor doesn't even wear underpants. That's what you'll be doing next. It starts with leg shaving and goes downhill from there. Well, just don't you bring any babies home to me. No sireee. I won't take any babies in here. That's all I can say."

I had been sitting at the dining room table, trying to study for an English test during this uproar about leg shaving. Kathy and Mary Ruth left the house heading for Walgreen's to buy a razor and blades with some of their baby-sitting money. Mommy walked over to me, leaned close and said, "Promise me, Laura. Promise me you'll never shave your legs. You have to promise you'll never do this to me."

She looked so desperate. It seemed so important to her that I said, "I promise, Mommy. I promise I won't shave my legs."

She patted me on the shoulder and said, "I knew I could count on you, sweetie."

I held out and kept my promise until this year, when I just didn't want to be the only eighth grade girl with hairy legs. I found a rusty old straight razor in the garage. It used to belong to Grampa Adams. I thought I could just shave my legs real quick right there. The blade was really sharp though, and I cut each leg twice so blood ran down my legs into my shoes. Now I have little scars where I messed up.

I thought about the scars on my legs from my first attempt at shaving. I didn't want to make any more promises to Mommy I couldn't keep. But I didn't want to turn against her. I didn't want to turn against my sisters either, but I had to say something. They were all looking at me, waiting for me to go one way or the other. Things were so quiet I swear I could hear each of us breathing.

"I'm not calling you a liar," I said. "Maybe you just don't remember turning them on."

"Oh, get out of here, scaredy cat," Kathy said.

"Yeah, little baby, mama's pet," Mary Ruth said.

"That's enough, all of you," Mommy said as she reached up, grabbed Kathy's radio, and threw it against the wall. It cracked open and fell to the plastic runner on the rug, batteries bouncing by my feet. "To hell with you and your stupid radios. You girls. Just you wait. Just you wait until this happens to you, and it will. Believe you me. I guarantee it. You don't know what pain is. You have no god damned idea, but you will, oh, you will, and when it hits you, when it really hits you, you'll be sorry. Oh, you'll be sorry. Mark my words. I hope you get treated just the way you're treating me."

"So do I because we're not doing anything wrong," Kathy said. "You are."

At that Mommy slammed her chair back to its upright position, rose awkwardly and wincing, as though in great pain, to her feet, and wobbled down the hall. We all followed her, uncertain what to do next. When she got to the door of her room, she turned to us, tears rolling down her cheeks, and said, "There, I hope you're happy, the three of you. You made your mother cry."

Then she stepped into her room and slammed the door. We shrank away from her muffled sobs. I was starting to feel guilty. I hadn't wanted to make her cry. We settled into Kathy's room without saying a word, Kathy on the bed, Mary Ruth and me on the floor facing her.

"It's not our fault that she's crying," Kathy said.

"We know that, right Laura?" Mary Ruth asked.

"I don't know; it feels really bad," I said.

"So what? Does she care about how we feel? No." Mary Ruth replied.

"I think she must care. She's our mother," I said.

"I've heard of dumb blondes, but this is ridiculous," Mary Ruth said to Kathy, pointing her finger at me. They both laughed. I got up and left the room. I walked down the hall and flopped down on my bed. I could hear Mommy sniffling in her room. And I prayed, "Oh, please, please God, make us normal."

This praying business doesn't seem to work though. I'm going to give it up. We get farther from normal every day. Kathy and Mary Ruth seem okay, but then I might seem that way too. And sometimes I am okay, level-headed and calm, no matter what's going on. But, oh, my mind just starts spinning and spinning sometimes, and I start shivering, and I can't stop.

I have to remind myself at times like this that things could be worse. I could have died the summer after fourth grade, the last time Mommy washed my hair. She used to wash our hair in the utility sink in the basement. It was never pleasant because the water was always scalding hot and even though we held washcloths over our eyes, stinging soapy water still seeped onto our eyeballs. But it got worse as we grew bigger. It got harder and harder for Mommy to get our heads right under the hot water flowing from the tap just the way she wanted. She started stuffing us down like jack-in-the boxes, except we were too big and strong for her hands, which were the lid. We kept popping up. So she'd shove down harder.

The very last time she washed my hair, she was running that hot, hot water on my head, while cramming my neck against the edge of the sink. The water was even hotter than usual. I screamed because it hurt so bad, and I tried to pull away. She said, "Stop your carrying on, Jesus, Mary, Joseph, I'm just washing your hair here." She pushed my neck harder against the edge of the sink.

I couldn't breathe. I'm not kidding. I really couldn't breathe. Other times when she'd washed my hair, it had hurt when she pushed me down against the sink, but my neck had never been pinned quite that way before, cutting off my windpipe. Then there was the feel of the water, hurting so bad too. She was wearing rubber gloves. How could she know how hot the water was?

She got shampoo on my scalp, and she scrubbed so hard it was like she was scouring off a thick layer of crud from a casserole dish that had baked too long. I could feel hate just pouring from her fingers, kneading into me, penetrating deep.

I wiggled and squirmed with all my might and managed to break away enough to get some air. Then she got a better grip on me and pushed me down harder. I screamed, "Let me go! Let me go!"

I let go of the washcloth, and soapsuds poured into my eyes. They burned my eyeballs, and I tried to wiggle every part of me away. Mommy crammed my neck up against the edge of the sink even harder and screamed, "Stop fighting me, Laura. Just you wait until your father hears about this."

I tried to say "I can't breathe," but when I opened my mouth water flowed into it. I just spit it out. I kicked and squirmed and thrashed about as fast and furious as I could, every so often managing to get my neck up far enough from the edge of the sink so that I could gulp some more air.

Then Grampa Adams came running up saying, "What's a goinga on herea, Laura. What area you doinga toa your mother?"

He grabbed my legs so I couldn't kick anymore. So I started lurching around with the trunk of my body sort of like a snake, and flailing my arms. All the while Mommy was still cramming my throat hard against the sink as she ran the hot water over my head again to rinse. They were both screaming at me, "Be quiet! Settle down! Behave yourself.! Wait until your father hears about this!"

On and on it went. It seemed like forever.

And then finally, Mommy and Grampa Adams plunked me down on the floor. I was so limp I almost couldn't stand up, but I stayed on my feet even though the room appeared to be moving slowly around me. Mommy grabbed a towel from a stack of them folded on the dryer by the sink and limped away. Grampa Adams grabbed a towel for himself and turned to walk away too. And I was there, dripping, every inch of me soaking wet. He turned around to face me from about six inches away, looked down at me with disgust and said, "Look what you've ah done to your mother and ah to me, gotten us soaking ah wet. See how exhausted she is? See how bad you've ah made her limp, you ah terrible, ungrateful child? You are ah very bad." And he stormed away.

I was glad to see him go. I didn't believe what he said. Even though I didn't die, I really couldn't breathe. I couldn't breathe, and it was one of the scariest times of my life. I figured nobody was going to convince me I was bad to fight for my life. Nobody. Mommy probably thought I could breathe the whole time. It's not like she was trying to kill me on purpose, but I was prepared to say something to Daddy if they brought it up at supper. The funny thing is neither of them said anything to him, and neither did I. And the good thing is that I didn't die.

Mommy said from then on we had to wash our own hair in the bathroom sink. The first time I washed my hair in the bathroom sink, I couldn't believe how nice it was—warm water on my scalp, my own fingers, washing carefully. No more hate. I wish we didn't have to worry about the water bill though ; I'd wash my hair once a week or more, and take showers too. We only get to bathe once a month, and Mommy says showers are absolutely out of the question. Too much water flushing right down the drain, the drain with her blood stain on it.

There are other things I can remind myself of too, like how lucky Kathy, Mary Ruth and I are that we haven't lost any fingers and toes due to frostbite from when we've had to walk home when the thermometer hits 17 below zero. I don't know how cold it would be considering the wind chill factor. I don't want to know. I remember last year, when I was in seventh grade, Mary Ruth and I got lucky on one of those way-below-zero days and got a ride to school after only walking about four or five blocks.

People always say when we're out in weather like that, "What are you girls doing? Don't you have enough sense to stay out of this cold?"

And we lie. We say something like, "Oh, we didn't know it would be this bad." We don't say, "Mommy's car is in the garage, but she won't ever use it to take us to school. She thinks it would make us lazy, and besides it would waste gas and cause unnecessary wear and tear on the car, even though she'll drive fifteen miles to buy day-old bread."

That cold, cold afternoon though, Mary Ruth and I weren't so lucky. We stayed after school to work on our school paper. By the time we walked out of the building, bundled up as much as we could be—our coats buttoned up tight, hats down as far as possible, scarves wrapped around our faces, leaving only a narrow strip for our eyes—there were no cars on the road. Everybody was inside, hiding from the bitter wind.

Even through my scarf, facing the wind, it hurt to breathe. It was so, so cold that Mary Ruth and I sometimes huddled in an alley at a garage door, thinking it might help us a little bit to be out of the wind, but it didn't help because it was so cold it was like the air was eating us alive. So we pressed on, and somehow we made it home. We had numb toes and fingers.

Kathy too. She'd walked to and from high school alone. It wasn't as far as the junior high school, but it was far enough to make a red ring with blisters on it where her boots had rubbed against her socks. We all had them. Mommy saw us huddling there by the heater vent in the hallway and said, "I don't know what you're carrying on so much for. Why when I was three years old my stepfather made me walk from one farm to another in Wisconsin in only a cotton dress and in my bare feet. This is nothing. It's good for you, makes you stronger."

She does think cold is good for us. She opens our bedroom windows about an inch in the winter after we've fallen asleep. Then, when she yanks our covers off to wake us up in the morning, it's so cold in the room I can see my breath in the air. But she won't let us close the windows or open the heat vent in our room. We have to get up fast and wince as our bare feet hit the cold tile floor. A lot of times we wake up with sore throats. If we complain she says, "Fresh air is good for you. Stop carrying on. If you don't like it, go live someplace where you think they'll treat you better."

I think winter is the worst. We can't just walk outside, take a long walk, clear our heads. And now here I am, riding back from church with Mommy, Kathy and Mary Ruth, bumbling through our third Christmas without Daddy. I count all the holidays like that throughout the year, starting with Thanksgiving, the first holiday that came along after his death. I think I should probably stop doing this. I'm sure it's wrong, but I don't know if I ever will stop. I did get myself to stop dreaming about him. I used to wake up each morning just drenched in this dreadful sorrow after dreaming that he was alive. So I started telling myself over and over when I was falling asleep. "You are not going to dream about Daddy. You are not going to dream about Daddy."

What happened after a couple weeks is that I stopped remembering my dreams. I don't know if I dream about him or not, but as long as I'm not running to him every night only to wake up to his death each day, that's an improvement. And a lot of times I forget completely who I am. Like just a little while ago at church. I sat in a pew with my hands resting on the soft wool of my reversible skirt. I've gotten a lot taller since Daddy bought it when I was in fourth grade, but I haven't gotten much wider, so every now and then I wear it with long, long knee socks to cover my legs. I can't wear it to school anymore because it's too far above my knees; I'd get sent home to change. But I knew nobody was about to send me home from church today. For a while as I sat in the pew, surrounded on all sides by rosy-cheeked, smiling people, it felt a little like Christmas is supposed to feel. And I felt safe and warm inside out.

Now, as we pull into our driveway, I don't feel as good, but I can still smell the evergreen sap of the three decorated trees in the sanctuary. Once inside, Kathy, Mary Ruth and I head to our rooms to change into slacks, and as though she's read our minds Mommy says, "Don't get too comfortable, girls, we're due at Downers Grove in an hour."

"Couldn't we just stay home, nice and cozy?" Kathy asks.

"Absolutely not. Christmas is a time to be with family," Mommy declares.

"The Rusas are not our family," Kathy says. "They're nice people and all, but it's not the same a having Gramma and Unc over. Why can't we have them over instead?"

"Yeah, like we used to do," I add. "We haven't spent one holiday with Gramma and Unc since before Daddy died."

"I don't have to answer to you, justify these decisions. We're leaving in half an hour."

"I'm not going," Mary Ruth says.

"Neither am I," Kathy says.

Mommy turns her gaze on me, "Are you coming, Laura?"

I don't say anything. I just wonder why things always have to be so hard with Mommy. Like she matters, and we don't matter at all. I feel like a charity case at the Rusas. I don't know why we can't just spend holidays with Gramma and Unc like we did before.

"Come on, honey, let's get ready now. I need to wrap a couple things to bring along," Mommy says, a sweet smile on her face. I wonder about that smile, enticing me, trying to swing me her way. How sincere is it really? If she really cared about me and Kathy and Mary Ruth, if she were really and truly our mother, wouldn't she want to see that we were happy, at least on Christmas?

"I don't want to go either," I blurt out.

"You what?" Mommy says, raising her voice.

"I want us to all be here together," I say.

"Fine, so you're just like your sisters now, are you, Laura? I'll go by myself, then."

"We don't want you to go by yourself. We want you to stay here with us," Kathy pleads.

"Yeah," Mary Ruth and I chime in.

"I'll go by myself and tell all the Rusas that you three girls think you're too good for them," Mommy threatens, storming into her room.

241

She comes out a few minutes later wearing lipstick and mascara and with her hair brushed off her face. She looks nicer than she has in quite a long time. She goes into the kitchen. We hear foil ripping and crunching as she wraps her offerings for the Rusas. Then she limps to the coat closet, pulls out a car coat I've just outgrown—the turquoise one with black collar, sleeves and pockets, the one I wore to Daddy's funeral. She puts it on, buttons it up, and steps outside into the cold.

"What do we do now?" I ask.

"I don't know. I think we should commemorate this occasion. The day we all stood up to Mommy together," Kathy says.

"Yeah," Mary Ruth says, "we were a united front."

"We should stick together all the time, you know, have a plan, to help us get through this," Kathy says.

"It should have a name, then, shouldn't it?" I ask.

"What should have a name?" Mary Ruth asks.

"Our plan," I say.

"Yes, a name. How about Plan X? She won't know what we're talking about if we say Plan X," Kathy suggests.

"Yeah, Plan X. The three of us sticking together," Mary Ruth says, "Let's shake on it."

We stand up facing each other in a little circle of three. We put our hands together in the middle, layering them palms down, and we shake our hands up and down and say, "Plan X, Plan X, Plan X, Plan X," until the muscles in our arms hurt too much for us to continue.

When we stop, I ask, "Now what are we going to do? How can we celebrate Christmas all by ourselves?"

"We'll have to think of something special," Mary Ruth says.

"Like cook our own dinner," Kathy suggests.

We all like that idea, but we know Mommy would have a fit if we take any of the food she is storing. Even though she has cans and cans of vegetables downstairs, at least two dozen cans of tuna fish on a shelf under the stove, two entire cabinet shelves full of cake mixes, one shelf full of assorted cereals, and an entire freezer stocked with food in the basement, she notices if even one little candy bar is taken. None of us knows how she can possibly keep track of it all, but she does. So we go to our rooms and sift through drawers, pockets, purses, looking for every piece of change we have. When we regroup at the dining room table we count out $3.87. We put on our coats, hats, scarves and boots, and set off for the Food Mart, a new store that is open seven days a week, including holidays.

A light snow starts falling, but the wind isn't blowing. The temperature is up in the 20s, so we are comfortable enough walking along the completely empty streets. When we reach the Food Mart we look in the frozen food section and find Salisbury steaks on sale for $.33 apiece, and frozen peas. They seem like the best ingredients for a meal. We load up. And there is a Sara Lee cheesecake. We grab that for dessert.

We take our goods up to the counter. Kathy pays in exact change. We have enough left over to buy some Tootsie Rolls, Mars Bars and Snickers too. As the tall, dark-haired man behind the counter bags our food and hands it to Kathy he says, "Merry Christmas, little waifs."

"Merry Christmas," we all say one after the other.

We begin laughing after we leave the store, calling each

other little waif this, little waif that. And we start singing Christmas carols, first the real ones and then goofy versions that have been going around at school for years like "We three kings of orient are puffing on a rubber cigar. It was loaded, it exploded, poof!" We all scatter at the poof, pretending to fall down. Then one after the other we slip on the ice and fall down for real. But we have on so many clothes, it doesn't hurt. We are laughing so hard, none of us can get up until the coldness of the ice starts seeping through our pants. I am thinking: see world, we can make our own Christmas, and it can be a happy one.

We help each other get to our feet and join arms, something we've never done before. We walk like that the rest of the way home. Once we get inside and into the kitchen, we pull out two dented but sturdy saucepans—one for the Salisbury steak, and one for the peas. We fill the pans with water, pull down Mommy's once famous fold-into-the-wall burners. We are in the process of pulling plastic pouches of frozen food from their cardboard boxes when in through the front door walks Mommy.

"What are you girls doing?" she asks as she slides open the coat closet door and pulls out a hanger.

"Don't worry we're not burning down the house," Kathy says.

"What are you doing?" Mary Ruth asks. "We thought you'd be gone longer. You must have really wolfed down your food."

"I couldn't relax and enjoy myself knowing you girls were here alone. Lord only knows what you might have already done. I just stopped in to say hi and give them some cookies and fudge. Then I drove straight home," she says, hanging up the car coat and slipping her see-through plastic boots off her wedgie canvas shoes.

"Want some Christmas dinner?" Kathy asks

"Let me see," Mommy says.

"No, go sit in your chair. We'll serve you," Kathy says.

"I don't like this, you girls having free rein in my kitchen," she replies.

"Oh, go on," Mary Ruth says. "It's Christmas. Let us cook our food and bring it to you."

"Please?" I ask.

"Oh, all right, but if you so much as leave one speck of dirt on my stove—"

"Oh, don't worry," Kathy says. "We'll leave everything nice and clean. I promise."

"Yeah, we promise," I say, knowing it was one promise we could keep.

So we eat our peas and Salisbury steak and Sara Lee cheesecake. It might not be turkey and all the trimmings, but it tastes good to us. Then Kathy, Mary Ruth and I start in on some chocolate fudge Mommy made that's loaded with marshmallows. Mommy sits down at her spinet. She sold the beautiful baby grand about a year ago. She said she was losing her touch and wasn't worthy of the baby grand anymore. I said that wasn't true and begged her to keep it, but she reminded me that Kathy, Mary Ruth and I no longer played, so we had no say in the matter. I couldn't argue. I quit after a talent show in sixth grade when I froze up while playing a mazurka. I ran off the stage and never wanted to play again. Oh, but listening to Mommy is as magical as ever. The little spinet doesn't have the fine tones that stir you to the bone like the baby grand did, but it sounds ever so pretty today.

Mommy plays the introduction to *Silver Bells*, and we all sing that in syncopated harmony. We'll probably sing through a whole book of carols and then maybe watch TV. There's bound to be some Christmas specials on. When it gets dark outside, we'll turn on our tree light. It's got this wheel of green, red, blue, and yellow. The colors rotate in front of a spotlight that shines on our aluminum tree. When Daddy first marched in with this artificial tree when I was nine, it was this wonderful and wacky thing. We were all in love with it and proud of Daddy for getting us something so modern. The next year we liked it too. But in 1960, the first Christmas after Daddy's death, the wheel started squeaking, and it was depressing to watch that color wheel turn. We've come to hate hauling it down from the attic. The branches are all twisted now and bunched up. But I guess you could say that's how our family is now too, so in a way it fits us to a T. Maybe next year we can talk Mommy into getting a real tree again. We could save up baby-sitting money to buy one if she'll let us. I know Kathy and Mary Ruth would be willing to do that.

This sure isn't the life I've been wishing for. But something about Plan X, our trip to the Food Mart and having Christmas at home again warms me up from the inside. My sisters were my surprise gift today, like the new clothes Daddy brought through the door so long ago, except maybe I don't have to worry about outgrowing them. I think together we can make the future better than the past.

Epilogue

It's been over half a century since the chilly Halloween afternoon when my mother took her last breath and kicked away the stool that stood between life and death, the known and the unknown. My sisters and I were at a costume party nearby. We came home in the darkening dusk and found her, but at ages two, three, and four, we didn't grasp the significance of the unresponsive body we encountered hanging by a rope from the basement beam. We didn't know what death was.

When our father came home, he promptly had us whisked away, without explanation, never to return to what was our first home, never to grieve with him and say farewell to the woman who gave us life. In the nine years he had left on this earth, I never once heard him say her name, Mary Agnes. It wasn't until about 25 years after her demise that I began to own my feelings about the elusive Mary Agnes and to integrate the abandoned girl inside of me with the stranger I had to become to carry on. It's been a long process.

Losing someone you love is always difficult, no matter what your age. The grief and longing, so emotionally jarring and even debilitating, can be triggered by anything—the whiff of lavender bath salts, the sight of autumn leaves falling outside a window, the feel of damp wool, the taste of chocolate milk. But to be baby-soft and just starting to piece the world together and to have those in charge of your upbringing do everything in their power to erase the very existence of someone you loved dearly can fracture a soul. In my adolescence it almost drove me insane.

My stepmother came on the scene a mere seven months after my mother's death. Shattered by the suicide, my father permitted my mother's parents to make decisions about how Kathy, Mary Ruth and I would be cared for while he recovered his equilibrium. They placed my sisters in an orphanage staffed by nuns they trusted implicitly. I would have gone, too, had I been a little bit older. And there was talk of our being adopted by different branches of the family. Finding a new wife and establishing what he thought was a normal home environment was my father's way of ensuring that no one would ever come close to splitting us up again.

The problem was that our stepmother enjoyed spending time with children in small doses, but she was not up to the actual demands of parenting. In an almost classic fairy-tale wicked-stepmother mode, she showed Kathy, Mary Ruth and me no mercy when we were alone with her, but when others were around she was charmingly quirky, even lovable. So at the time of my father's death, there was the whammy of the loss—and this time I knew exactly what death was in all of its dark and dreadful finality, talk of God's will and meeting up in Heaven notwithstanding—plus the stepmother who was out of place in an affluent community, out of touch with our needs as well as her own, out of control in terms of the emotional abuse she dished out with relish, and going out of her mind with anger and grief and bitterness at just about every person and thing, living and dead. Not a good combination.

After Kathy, Mary Ruth and I made our pact to thwart our stepmother's brand of totalitarianism, things got worse before they got better. We were young. We had not been treated well. Our little jealousies and competitions didn't just instantly disappear. Our stepmother was never able to accept less than a dictatorial role when we lived under her roof, and her escalating tirades as we tried to do ordinary things like attend basketball games, go to slumber parties, and talk to boys on the phone drove each of us to ultimately spend more nights on the floors and couches of friends' houses than we did in our own beds.

Once when I came home after window-shopping instead of washing her car, she was so irate that she chased me around the house with a large kitchen knife in hand. She was just under five feet tall, and I'd gone through a growth spurt, so I was about six inches taller than she was. As she sputtered at me, I finally noticed how small she was. I stopped running and put my hand on her forehead, knowing that she might slash my arm. But my touch jolted her. She blinked, closed her mouth, lowered the knife, and stomped away. After that I was never afraid of what she might do to me physically. I was more afraid of what I might do to her.

There were countless times when she'd be inching her way up the basement stairs with a can of tuna or peas in hand, and she'd call to me, angrily, impatiently. As soon as I got to the top of the stairs, she'd start in on what a miserable excuse I was for a daughter, how I didn't care about anyone except myself, and she'd grow louder and more vehement with each step. I can't tell you how many times it crossed my mind to just shove her back down the stairs once she reached the top. It wasn't my conscience or anything like that stopping me. It was the thought that I'd probably end up incarcerated for a long time if I acted on this urge to just silence her once and for all.

And it was the '60s, a time when promises of adventure, new beginnings and a better world seemed to flow from the very air we breathed. Enchantment came from everywhere— the radio, TV, periodicals and especially the voices of our friends. Ah, those friends, and the music, and the poetry, and the drugs, and the laughter, and the wild, wild times. My sisters chose their activities more wisely than I. They set goals. They won scholarships. They stayed focused. I did the opposite. And it seemed each decision I made was worse than the last until by the time I was 19 years old, I was convinced I'd completely ruined my life. I was limp, half alive, and it was then that my sisters picked me up, and despite the fact that they themselves were wounded, they carried me until I learned to hope again.

And things improved. The darkest hours passed. Years later, when it was time to tell my own daughter about my mother's suicide, she asked me why her grandmother didn't want to live, and I said that I'll never really know, but I think she simply forgot that things would get better. It takes living through cycles over time to fully know that things will always change—your tastes, feelings, insights even your sense of self and your most cherished beliefs change as you find yourself facing situations you never dreamed you'd see. That's worth sticking around for. But many of us forget. And many of us leave children behind.

It is that child left behind who drove me to write this book. As I typed installment loan contracts on an IBM Selectric in a downtown Chicago high rise when my footloose contemporaries reveled in the Woodstock mud; as I stood shivering on the shores of Lake Michigan saying "I do" with a man I didn't love because I didn't have the courage to leave him; as I pulled out a spiral notebook and tried to find myself in the pages, the little girl inside of me begged me to give her life. But I thought: who do you think you are to imagine ever doing something like that?

Later, as I began a new life with one duffle bag and the clothes on my back; opened a tent flap to see goats picking orange peels from the beach of Morocco's Agadir; sat in the kitchen of a chilly London flat and wrote my grandmother a long-overdue love letter, which reached her shortly before she died; sat on a bench in Chicago's Art Institute and lost track of time looking at an enormous black painting with an orange stripe on the side; the little girl inside me begged again to be brought to life. I wrote some clumsy poems, and left it at that.

As I embraced San Francisco's idiosyncrasies just before every last guy with any brain cells left cut his long locks; as I bought an old Kohler upright piano for $17 per month and spent hours on its bench trying to write songs; the girl called to me strong and insistent. But I didn't listen. I had other things to do, especially after I fell in love with a divorced father of two boys, became a stepparent in a blue-collar family, and shortly thereafter the mother of a beautiful baby girl.

Laura McHale Holland

And much happened in the world over the years. There were many good things, certainly, but so many problems, too, and so few solutions—massacres, famines, and floods; cancer claiming victims at younger and younger ages; global warming; the AIDS epidemic; too many people in rumpled clothes standing in the rain on too many corners for too many years holding too many cardboard signs saying, "Homeless. Will work for food"; steadily decreasing funding for social programs and schools; the ever widening gap between the average worker's pay and salaries of those at the top; escalating health care costs; globalization and the black holes left where, each year, more jobs have gone offshore; terrorism on our shores and around the world, and yet more war, and so many lives lost.

Sometimes when feeling powerless in the face of all of this, I've told the girl inside that compared to the lives of so many people on the planet, I am living in the lap of luxury. I have a front door to unlock, a closet for my clothes. I have food in the refrigerator and loved ones to enjoy it with. I told the girl left behind to scram and remember that most of all I'm just plain lucky to be alive. And scram she did, sometimes for a month, sometimes for years, but she always came back, wanting to be heard.

Occasionally between my efforts to make a decent living, between the nursery rhymes, field trips and parent-teacher conferences, occasionally I'd take a stab at writing about my formative years, but I always petered out after a page or two of pretty good prose. I never made a commitment to follow the project through. Then, finally, a few years ago, I realized the little girl calling to me wasn't going away. She would keep pestering me, and if I didn't listen and write now, she would probably be pestering me still when it came time for me to leave this world. I decided I'd rather take care of her and see what came next. So I did.

Once I began, I was filled with the desire to—as honestly and accurately as it is possible for an adult looking back to do—plumb the depths of my root experiences, say the things I could not say at the time due to a combination of limited vocabulary and fear, and convey my very real thoughts, feelings and observations. I wanted to let people experience it as I did, without the reference points an adult enjoys. I think I have done this, and it has given the lost little girl in me some peace. She is no longer calling to me.

Kathy, Mary Ruth and I remain lifelong best friends and live within 100 miles of each other in the San Francisco Bay Area. Our father didn't live to see it, but his wish that we remain together came true both in our physical proximity and in our bonded spirits. By now we have enjoyed good times too numerous to count. We began like three castaways on a homemade raft, trying to navigate in high winds and rain with no knowledge, instruments, fresh water or even nourishing food. Now we are on solid ground, each accomplished in her own right and trying, each in her own way, to make a positive difference in the world, no matter how small.

When I was 17 years old, I thought I'd left my stepmother and Hinsdale behind for good. Kathy and Mary Ruth had similar sentiments when they left before me. But return we all did, for visits. We nicknamed our stepmother Little Ma, and she was usually glad to see us drop by or chat on the phone, as long as we didn't ask anything of her. She also relished playing the role of the sweet, suffering, abandoned widow and never passed up an opportunity to tell friends, neighbors and relatives how heartless we were. She continued her physical and mental deterioration. She was diagnosed with multiple sclerosis. Her limp worsened. She walked with great effort, sometimes leaning on walls for support, and sometimes shuffling slowly behind a metal walker. She also developed glaucoma and was blind in the last decade or so of her life.

Kathy, Mary Ruth and I never talked with her about how she abused us; she just wasn't capable of that sort of interaction. We had each realized long ago we had to let go of the notion that she would ever function as a parent for us, and later we did our best to forgive her. We came to realize that her actions were the result of the ways she had been mistreated in her childhood. She never had a chance to heal, and so she passed the pain on. It happens in families all the time. I waited until I was well into my 30s to take on the job of parenting. I waited until I could trust myself to not pass the pain on to another generation.

One of Little Ma's greatest fears was that she would end up in a nursing home, and she clung to her little redwood house as it fell into disrepair. The day before I moved to California I paid her a visit. I washed her hair, and she said while I was massaging her scalp, "Laura, you are so gentle, you know, you are beautiful inside and out." I was stunned. She'd never said anything like that to me before. Then she confided that she'd always expected I would be the one who would stay home and care for her and that is what she'd raised me for. I didn't say anything. I just rinsed her hair. Then as I was wrapping her hair in a warm towel, she begged me not to go to the West Coast. "I'll come back and visit," I said. Then a familiar snide tone came into her voice, "What do you think I married a man with three children for if it wasn't to have someone to take care of me when I got old?" I helped her over to her well-worn reclining chair and I said, "Well, maybe you should have done it for love, Little Ma." She plopped down in her favorite spot, sighed, and replied, "How about you make yourself useful and see if there's something to eat in the fridge."

It took me years to stop feeling remorse about leaving her. And that came largely as a result of my realizing the intense, overwhelming feelings I thought I had for Little Ma were really misplaced feelings I have for my real mother. This freed me to see that I have no obligation to the woman my father picked out in a rush, the woman who gave little and expected everything in return, the woman who belittled me almost from the day we met. It freed me to love her anyway, but in a more measured way, to feel compassion for her plight and tenderness for the good times we shared, and appreciation for her tasteless sense of humor and her fierce, determined nature. But to somehow not be too worried about her situation.

Little Ma did end up in a nursing home, a very good one that Kathy flew back to Illinois to find for her. And the sale of the house she clung to so desperately paid for most of the years she spent there. Living in an institution turned out to be much better than she thought it would be. She met and fell in love with a gentle, easygoing man. He adored her in a way I think my father never did, and together they made each other whole. They got married, and in her last couple of years of life she had the gift of peace.

I have had the gift of time, friendship, family, and so many resources. For decades now I've lived the normal sort of life I used to dream of having as a child. Normal in the sense that I'm not plagued by internal demons; I'm living in the present, taking care of business as it comes. My husband is steadfast and true, our daughter is healthy and happy, my two stepsons are fine and loving individuals. And I live in one of the most beautiful places on the planet. Just looking into the yard now as birds flock to the feeder by my window is a bit of heaven.

In my cluttered office I have a few mementos from my early days. A picture of my grandmother that used to hang on her dining room wall reminds me of her unconditional love; a snapshot of my parents all gussied up and holding hands and smiling into the sun as they sat on the steps of her childhood home reminds me that there was more to their story than its tragic end; a French provincial lamp my mother picked out for our long-ago living room, a keepsake that Unc stored for years and then refurbished and shipped to Kathy, Mary Ruth and me, reminds me that he has never forgotten how important our connection to our mother is.

It is my hope that those who read this will be reminded of the depth and complexity of children. No matter how things appear to an outside observer, one never knows what the child is really experiencing at home. We hope for the best, but can't truly know. A life of abuse and neglect is the only reality some children ever know, and they don't easily reveal their despair to others. They will, in fact, do their best to appear like they need no help at all because it is too painful to admit otherwise, even to themselves.

I hope this book has given you something you can use. A kind word, a hug, a pleasant afternoon passed without incident are little gifts that a young one stores and draws upon for strength when the time is right to face, and ultimately overcome, the reality of abandonment and abuse. If you remember this, then I will have made a small contribution with this endeavor.

With all good wishes,
Laura McHale Holland

Laura McHale Holland

Acknowledgements

Thanks to my beloved husband, Jim, whose honesty, verve and constant acts of kindness make day-to-day life such a joy; our daughter, Moira, wiser than her years and a fiercely loyal friend to many, including me; my stepsons, Ryan, who never fails to be kind, and Jackson, who always fights for what is right—they are fine young men who tickle my funny bone and make me proud. Thanks to my sisters: Kathy, who embodies creativity, generosity and spunk, and who designed the cover of this book; and Mary Ruth, a loyal confidante and brilliant beauty who works ceaselessly to improve the lives of working people everywhere. And thanks to my steadfast Uncle John, a sweetheart like no other. The happy times I continue to have with these people give me courage to seek the truth, even when it's painful.

Thanks also to The Storytelling Association of California, in particular Ruth Stotter, from whom I learned so much about finding the heart of a story and then getting out of the way to let its message come through. To Sally Smith, a community journalist par excellence who taught me the importance of being vigilant about every detail. To Claire

Blotter, Susan Ford and Lee Jenkins, fine writers all, who helped me through this book's first draft. To Eileen Hayes, long-time best bud who has always encouraged my creative efforts. To Karen Batchelor for her generous help with editing. To Jo-Anne Rosen for her copyediting and layout assistance. And to Troy Vera for his work on the layout and his charming chapter icon illustration.

And thanks to Nanos Valaoritis, renowned surrealist poet and professor emeritus of comparative literature and creative writing at San Francisco State University. His nonlinear approach to work freed me to follow wherever my mind leads. And thanks to novelist Larry Heinemann. Long ago, as a story workshop leader at Columbia College in Chicago, he told me, "Laura, you are a writer. All you have to do is do it." To do it, though, you have to believe in yourself, and that took me decades.

Laura McHale Holland's fiction, features and essays have appeared in such publications as *The Best of Every Day Fiction Three*, *Vintage Voices*, *NorthBay biz* magazine, the *Noe Valley Voice* and the original *San Francisco Examiner*. Her memoir *Reversible Skirt* won the annual RockWay Press International Writing Competition.

Laura currently heads the editorial department of a trade publication covering the electronic payments industry. She also belongs to Redwood Writers and the Storytelling Association of California. To keep up with her, please visit http://lauramchaleholland.com.